ALL THINGS ARE POSSIBLE TO BELIEVERS

ALL THINGS ARE POSSIBLE TO BELIEVERS

*Reflections on the Lord's Prayer
and the Sermon on the Mount*

RUDOLF SCHNACKENBURG

Translated by James S. Currie

WESTMINSTER JOHN KNOX PRESS
Louisville, Kentucky

Translated from *Alles kann, wer glaubt: Bergpredigt und Vaterunser in der Absicht Jesu,* © Verlag Herder, Freiburg im Breisgau, 1984, new edition 1992

English translation © 1995 Westminster John Knox Press

Book design by Drew Stevens
Cover design by Tanya R. Hahn

First edition

Published by Westminster John Knox Press
Louisville, Kentucky

This book is printed on acid-free paper that meets the American National Standards Institute Z39.48 standard. ∞

PRINTED IN THE UNITED STATES OF AMERICA

95 96 97 98 99 00 01 02 03 04 — 10 9 8 7 6 5 4 3 2 1

Library of Congress Cataloging-in-Publication Data

Schnackenburg, Rudolf, date.
    [Alles kann, wer glaubt. English]
    All things are possible to believers / Rudolf Schnackenburg. — 1st ed.
        p.   cm.
    Includes index.
    ISBN 0-664-25517-5 (alk. paper)
    1. Sermon on the mount.   2. Lord's prayer.   I. Title.
  BT380.2.S32513   1995
    226.9'06—dc20   94-22146

CONTENTS

PREFACE

THE QUESTION OF HOW we can understand the Sermon on the Mount with its extreme demands and how we can put it into practice in a world filled with evil, and with evil thoughts and desires on the rise in the human heart, remains a storm center for all Christians. This book had its origins in the peace discussion of the 1970s and 1980s. If the peace movement today has taken significant steps forward, if all tensions are being reduced and nations have moved closer to one another, even then by no means has everything been achieved that Jesus desired in his message of the inbreaking of God's kingdom. As important as the establishment of peace is in the personal, social, and political realms, there are still other themes that are addressed in the programmatic speech of Jesus, such as our relationship to worldly possessions, relief to the poor and oppressed, veracity and faithfulness, sexual purity and discipline, and spirituality and forgiveness of sins. The Sermon on the Mount excludes no area of life and places every human being before the countenance of God. Thus the question forces itself over and over again: Who can put it into practice? Is it not all unrealistic, utopian, and illusionary?

Perhaps in this regard it will help to reflect on the Lord's Prayer, which exposes Jesus' aims and yet at the same time deals with the needs and fears that oppressed human beings then and do so now. In his book on the prayer of our Lord (Freiburg im Breisgau, 4th ed., 1981), Heinz Schürmann calls it a "key to understanding Jesus." Thus I wish to try to juxtapose, and as far as possible to examine together, the two texts that are of interest to Jesus and yet are distinct in kind. The Lord's Prayer stands at the center of the Sermon on the Mount!

This book arose out of lectures and studies that are listed in its first edition (Freiburg im Breisgau, 1984). It did not seem necessary to alter the text very much for this publication. The theme "All things are possible to the one who believes" retains its sense of urgency, which is challenge, courage, and trust.

RUDOLF SCHNACKENBURG

ALL THINGS ARE POSSIBLE TO BELIEVERS

INTRODUCTION: AN EXTRAORDINARILY BOLD WORD (MARK 9:23)

A STATEMENT IS HANDED DOWN to us from Jesus that is disconcerting in its absoluteness and its bold promise: "All things are possible to the one who believes." But it corresponds to the attitude of Jesus as it appears throughout the Gospels. He reveals a disarming trust in God the Father that is shaken by nothing, and he attempts to quicken this trust in his disciples. His effort to instill it in his disciples is confirmed by another statement that is consciously formulated in an extreme fashion and with exaggerated imagery: "Truly, I say to you, whoever says to this mountain, 'Be taken up and cast into the sea,' and does not doubt in his heart, but believes that what he says will come to pass, it will be done for him" (Mark 11:23).

Whence does Jesus have this absolute certainty? He himself is profoundly filled with it in his relationship with God! In the context of that statement of faith, that all things are possible—namely, in the story of the healing of the epileptic boy (Mark 9:14–27)—it can hardly refer to anyone other than Jesus himself. The disciples have vainly tried to free the sick son of the distressed father from his suffering. When Jesus enters, the situation is explained to him and he cries out, "O faithless generation, how long am I to be with you? How long am I to bear with you?" The boy suffers another attack when he is brought to Jesus. The desperate father asks Jesus, "If you can do anything, have pity on us and help us." Jesus seizes on the hidden doubt and replies, "If you can! All things are possible to the one who believes." Then he heals the boy. The father doubts the power of Jesus, and Jesus' answer, anticipating his healing of the boy, can scarcely refer to anything but the faith of Jesus which makes this possible for him. We should not take offense at the

I

perhaps surprising expression that Jesus speaks of *his* faith—unique in the Gospels, but compare Heb. 12:2, "Jesus the pioneer and perfecter of our faith." It is absolute confidence that the Father will grant him everything for which he asks (cf. John 11:22 and 41f.). That was the innermost connection of the earthly Jesus whose human existence we must take seriously.

Immediately following the healing of the epileptic boy is a brief exchange between Jesus and his disciples, who were unable to heal the boy. The conversation betrays the preoccupation of the primitive church with the story as it has been handed down. The disciples ask Jesus, "Why could we not cast out the demon?" Jesus replies, "This kind cannot be driven out by anything but prayer" (Mark 9:28f.). Two aspects of this answer are noteworthy: No part of the statement that the believer can do all things is retracted; yet it is now extended to the disciples (and the later church). At the same time, however, it is also explained: When scandalous things are demanded of the believer, the believer must engage in prayer, prayer that knows no doubt. This corresponds precisely to that other statement in Mark 11:23 which profoundly influenced the primitive church as "mountain moving" faith (cf. 1 Cor. 13:2). In Mark 11:24, another statement is added regarding prayer: "Therefore I tell you, whatever you ask in prayer, believe that you have received it, and it will be yours." This prayer, which assumes fulfillment and which Jesus teaches his disciples, is passed down in different words that were precious to the primitive church (Matt. 7:7–11; par. Luke 11:9–13; Matt. 18:19; cf. John 14:13; 15:7; 16:23). Thus the statement with which we began, "All things are possible to the one who believes," also applies to Jesus' disciples and to all who pray in his Spirit and in communion with him (by praying in his "name").

An extraordinarily bold word, many Christians would say, for have we not often had the sense that our fervent prayers were not heard? Even in the primitive church there were clearly such objections. In 1 John 5:14 we find a certain qualification: "And this is the confidence which we have in him [God], that if we ask anything *according to his will* he hears us." We cannot treat here the whole problematic of the prayer that is certain of fulfillment. But more often than not, does not some doubt creep into our prayers and requests? Must we not also consider the content of our requests? Do we not pray in the Lord's Prayer, "*Thy* will be done"?

Only one thing should become clear here: Jesus himself was deeply convinced of the power of God, which surpasses all human measures, and was filled with an insuperable trust that God will help, heal, and save. It is the inner source of Jesus' whole proclamation, and everything that he says to his disciples and demands of them rests on that. Without this trust which is directed to God, Jesus' message cannot be understood, is not acceptable, and cannot be converted into action.

If the statement "All things are possible to the one who believes" is read apart from this basic presupposition, it is subject to dangerous misunderstanding. The believer cannot do "all things" by his or her own strength. It is not what the believer "achieves" by means of his or her faith that leads to success; rather, it is the power of God which the believer summons through faith and prayer. It is God who brings about what is humanly impossible (cf. Mark 10:27). The believer borrows, as it were, the arm of God and is thereby able to perform "wonders." The human being is only one who cries out, but in his or her trust in God, the believer cries out with such a powerful voice that God hears in accordance with his pledge and his promise. God has given us this pledge in Jesus Christ who embodies this trust in his person at all points in his life. God himself provided the final confirmation that he hears the fervent cry of his Son "with loud cries and tears" (Heb. 5:7) when he raised the crucified one from the dead.

This scandalous *trust* that inspired Jesus himself and that he desired to awaken in his disciples appears to me also to be a key to understanding the Sermon on the Mount, in which Jesus' extreme demands astound and irritate us. But they do not stand alone; they must be read in the context of Jesus' whole message and proclamation. The basis out of which they arose must be examined: only then do they become comprehensible, bearable, and practicable. They are intimately related to, and bear the innermost contact with, the statement that all things are possible to the one who believes. For this statement is also offensive, but at the same time it encourages us to risk the utmost.

The chief feature of Jesus' thought appears even more strongly in the Lord's Prayer than in the Sermon on the Mount. It bears direct witness to Jesus' fundamental trust in the Father which he wished to bring to his disciples. At the same time it is not blind to the concrete needs, dangers, and temptations to which we are exposed in our earthly existence. On the contrary, by this trust in God the Father we are given the ability to withstand all trials and perplexities and to confront the power of evil. The Lord's Prayer itself is indeed a prayer that should be prayed

with the conviction that "all things are possible to the one who believes." Whoever understands this statement will also pray the Lord's
Prayer in the right spirit.

The Sermon on the Mount and the Lord's Prayer can be mutually
understood. From the one we must constantly glance at and listen to
the other in order to understand each of these texts. But even more,
hearing the Sermon on the Mount, we must engage in prayer to the
Lord; and praying the Lord's Prayer, we must always bear in mind what
Jesus' Sermon on the Mount demands. Thus, with their constant contact and interrelationship we will now attempt to examine more closely
the Sermon on the Mount and the Lord's Prayer.

PART I. THE SERMON ON THE MOUNT

I. THE INSUPERABLE
SERMON ON THE MOUNT

THE WINNER OF THE PEACE PRIZE of the German book trade in 1981, Russian and student of the German language Lev Kopelew, described the Sermon on the Mount in his impressive speech as the "highest, the purest height achievable by the human spirit." The message of peace, he said, rang out at first only for a few listeners. It was heard by the poor, the suffering, degraded, defenseless persons in a tiny country. "But since then it has reached hundreds of millions of persons on all continents. No rumors of war, no subtle reinterpretations have been able to distort its true spirit. For these words of love and peace are unequivocal."[1] As honest and moving as Kopelew's speech is, we must still ask, Are the words of the Sermon on the Mount unequivocal? In fact, they have been variously interpreted; we need only consider the burning questions today of the maintenance and preservation of peace.

In early 1983 the Catholic television editor Franz Alt published a little book (Eng. trans., 1985: *Peace Is Possible: The Politics of the Sermon on the Mount*) that has become a best-seller.[2] In it he writes: "You don't have to be a theologian to grasp the meaning and the spirit of the Sermon on the Mount. . . . Jesus spoke not only to theologians, but to the people. And *all* people are meant, in *all* walks of life. No Christian can sidestep the Sermon on the Mount. It contains the essence of Christianity. If you meditate on it intensively enough, you won't need anyone to interpret it for you. You have to take the words as they are written."

Whoever reads this little book further will not doubt that Franz Alt is guided by a strong Christian commitment. But he is a political journalist and wishes to apply Jesus' demands to the actual discussion of

7

peace. His theme, "Our religious, private, and political existence is inseparable," cannot be challenged. But we may ask whether the concrete consequences that he sees prove to be true in the same way. Recent experience teaches us that politics is not separable from religion, especially in Muslim states. Religious fanaticism can lead to conquests and wars; often the love of peace cannot prevent armed conflicts. The application of Jesus' ethical demands succumbs to momentary relationships and how one judges them. With similar religious seriousness, other Christians reach conclusions different from those of Alt.[3] Thus, he proceeds with the exegetes and becomes himself a commentator, even in his new book on the "first new human being." As stimulating as much of it is, much may be disputed. Can the text of the Sermon on the Mount be read "literally"? It does not directly address the problems that afflict us today. The sayings of Jesus must always be set in their immediate historical context. There are, however, strong impulses that emanate from them; they confront the individual in his or her condition and society in its constantly changing structure.

A commentary for today on the sayings of Jesus collected in the Sermon on the Mount is indispensable and unavoidable. How should we then proceed? With sayings of *Jesus,* we must interpret them in *his* spirit, according to *his* intention. Thus the Sermon on the Mount cannot be treated as an isolated document; rather, one must take into account Jesus' entire proclamation and his own behavior. As will be demonstrated, the Sermon on the Mount in the Matthean and Lukan forms already reflects an interpretation and application of collected sayings of Jesus through early preachers and evangelists. We can assume that they were closely associated with the spirit of Jesus, and we can test this by means of the rich material they pass on as the words and deeds of Jesus outside the Sermon on the Mount. With this broader basis, we must attempt to approach as nearly as possible Jesus' original intention. Only then will we not run the risk of imputing our own thoughts and wishes to Jesus.

That is indeed no simple task. Throughout the centuries Christians have struggled for the true meaning. Even the "literal" meaning has a prehistory. The words of the activist Franz Alt remind me of the confession of another Christian of the last century influenced by the Sermon on the Mount, Count Leo Tolstoy, who in his confession *What I Believe* (1884) writes very similarly: If Christianity has had so little effect even up to today, it is a consequence of the fact that Jesus' demands have been diluted and shoved aside. Tolstoy also claimed that the words of Jesus should be taken literally and converted into action. For him, the heart of the matter is the commandment not to resist evil. Regarding Matt. 5:38f., he writes, "Do not resist evil means: Never use force!" He pursues the consequences of this idea and rejects the whole notion of the state, which is constructed on the basis of force.[4]

Franz Alt and others who are active today in the cause of peace do not wish to go that far. That leads to anarchy: We must remember the catastrophic uses of force in the Russian empire in Tolstoy's day. Subjective assumptions are also at work in his commentary on the Sermon on the Mount: The social relationships led him to an interpretation that must first be examined in the light of the intention and activity of Jesus in the tradition as a whole.

According to the witness of the Gospels, there is no doubt that Jesus acknowledged the civil order and did not fundamentally attack the state's authority (cf. Mark 12:17). His criticism of the rulers' misuse of power (Mark 10:42) does not make him a revolutionary or freedom fighter but rather places the disciples under obligation to another "basic law," namely, that of serving one another in love (Mark 10:43f.). His aim was a "revolution of the heart," which certainly Count Tolstoy also intended but for which he lost sight of all measures and limitations in the earthly realm. Against the charge that this opened the door for complete anarchy, Tolstoy replied that, on the contrary, if all people fulfilled the demands of the Sermon on the Mount, paradisiacal conditions would prevail on earth.

On this point we are perplexed. Will there ever be a time when all people fulfill the demands of the Sermon on the Mount? Will paradisiacal conditions ever come about on earth? In view of the evil that appears over and over again in history, and the frightening horror inflicted by human beings on others, and in view of our own experience today in which oppression, terror, and murder are prevalent and still on the rise, we can hardly answer this question in the affirmative. But this only forces us back to the fundamental question, Must or can we only take the text of the Sermon on the Mount as it stands, namely, literally? The real and still unelaborated problem of the Sermon on the Mount is how we may understand the extreme demands of Jesus, these radical demands, and implement them in the reality of our world.

There are two poles in tension: the new order that God wills to bring about with his kingdom, and the existing old world in which we human beings are held fast and must live. How did Jesus himself see this tension, and how did he propose to resolve it? How are we to conduct ourselves in this world according to his instructions? Throughout the centuries these questions have engaged, disturbed, and distressed Christianity. The pendulum has constantly swung back and forth between these two poles: full realization of Jesus' demands or relative fulfillment in the reality of this world. A final answer has not been found; even today this fundamental problem remains insuperable.

We wish to make clear the "insuperable Sermon on the Mount" with an overview of its history of interpretation. We can then be more thoughtful as we seek an answer from the spirit of Jesus as to his intention.

THE HISTORY OF INTERPRETATON
TO THE ENLIGHTENMENT

The early church was convinced that Jesus' radical demands were doable and must be realized. However, in the New Testament, the aftereffect of Jesus' words and the reaction to Jesus' action are discernible. In Romans, Paul writes, "Bless those who persecute you; bless and do not curse them. . . . Repay no one evil for evil, but take thought for what is noble in the sight of all. If possible, so far as it depends upon you, live peaceably with all. . . . Do not be overcome by evil, but overcome evil with good" (Rom. 12:14–21). Paul expressly demands that they live in peace with all people. He is thinking not only of the church but also of outsiders and those far off. He does indeed add, "if possible," by which he intends no circumscription on the part of the peace-seeker but rather insurmountable obstacles on the part of others. Yet he does not mention conflicts between peoples and nations. That was not an issue, since there was relative peace in the empire at that time (the Pax Romana). In addition, the young Christian churches had no political influence.

The ancient *Teaching of the Twelve Apostles* (the *Didache*), from the early second century, describes the way of life and the way of death. The way of life begins with the central commandment of love, to which the Golden Rule and the command to love one's enemies were added. Still other demands of the Sermon on the Mount are then treated (*Di-*

dache 1). Throughout the juxtaposition of this with the way of death, it becomes clear that only by fulfilling all commands may one enter life. But Jesus' radical demands are, at the same time, set in the reality of our world. At the end we read: "See that no one leads you away from this way of teaching, because he will lead you away from God. For if you are able to bear the whole yoke of the Lord, you will be perfect. But if you are unable to do that, then do what you can" (*Did.* 6.1–2). A certain mitigation, a certain concession to human weakness is unmistakable. Later that will become an objection to the Catholic interpretation as it has endured through the centuries in various forms.

Nonetheless, in the command to love our enemies, we see how deeply it has taken root in the hearts of Christians. In the middle of the second century the philosopher and martyr Justin quotes the commandment to love one's enemies along with other admonitions of the Sermon on the Mount (*Apol.* 15.9–17). In the dialogue with the Jew Trypho, he applies it to his relationship to Jews: "We do not hate you, but we pray that if you are not converted, you will all find mercy in the sympathetic and mercy-rich Father" (*Dialogue with Trypho* 108.3; cf. 96.3; 133.6).

In contrast, the words of nonjudgmentalism and of repeated forgiveness were interpreted in the early church in terms of the inter-Christian, brotherly community.[5] The oldest extant Christian sermon, the so-called *Second Letter of Clement,* calls to repentance those Christians who always talk about the words of the Lord but who never reflect them in action, and threatens with divine judgment those who in this way desecrate and make foolish the name of Christ among the heathen (2 *Clem.* 13.17).

In his writing *On Patience,* Tertullian takes Jesus' saying that one must forgive one's brother seventy times seven and joins it to many statements from the Sermon on the Mount, making it a fundamental demand for all Christians. This emphasis on forgiveness and reconciliation recognizes a basic idea of the Sermon on the Mount: to be merciful as God shows mercy to us (Luke 6:36). That is also the spirit of the Lord's Prayer, for there we pray, "Forgive us our debts as we forgive our debtors." For Clement of Alexandria, brotherly forgiveness becomes an expression of love of one's enemies.[6]

We have Augustine to thank for the oldest separate treatment of the Matthean version of the Sermon on the Mount. This two-part

work, *De sermone Domini in monte,* comes out of his early period
(393–94) and provides a continuous exegesis that perhaps disappoints
us today but that contains a warm spirituality. The church father is
moved most—as was all of Christian antiquity—by the beatitude
regarding the pure in heart. It was the great desire of the people of that
time to see God. Augustine understands the beatitude regarding the
peacemakers only in terms of inner peace. At the end of the first part
(Matthew 5) he asks who can do this, and he answers: only the one who
is fully and completely merciful. Like Tertullian, he also emphasizes this
basic demand which is measured against God's behavior. The church
fathers were very conscious of the relationship between God's behavior
which is manifested in Jesus and the behavior required of us.

The most significant commentary on Matthew's Gospel in antiquity comes from John Chrysostom. In it the later bishop of Constan-
tinople maintains that Jesus himself fulfilled the law and desires the
same of us. The character of the whole world shall be changed. Gradu-
ally we can realize the commandment to love our enemies. With "the
law of the Spirit" (Rom. 8:1f.), that is, by the Holy Spirit, we are given
greater assistance to fulfill in a new way the intent of the law.[7] The great
admirer of Paul learned from that apostle that what we are unable to do
with our own strength becomes achievable through life in Christ Jesus
which comes from the Holy Spirit.

How strongly the words of the Sermon on the Mount engaged life
and moved hearts can be seen in asceticism and monasticism. If various
motives may have contributed to this considerable movement, the An-
chorites and the Cenobites were influenced by Jesus' words the most.
For these first monks, the admonition not to judge became a practical,
ascetic rule which was enjoined repeatedly. As Bishop Paphnutius reports, he implored his spiritual father, Makarius, "Speak to me!" The
latter said, "Harm no one and judge no one; observe that, and you will
live."[8]

But was this withdrawal from the world not also an indication that
Jesus' demands could scarcely be realized in the world? In the course of
the history of interpretation, it has often been noted that the radical demands of the Sermon on the Mount are only for monks to fulfill. Is the
Sermon on the Mount simply a special ethic for an elite group, for the
"perfect" or for those striving for perfection? Is it not also valid for people of the world, even for responsible persons in society, for politicians
and national leaders?

A Twofold or Two-Story Ethic?

Now and then we encounter the notion that the Sermon on the Mount is directed only at a small circle of Jesus' disciples. It first appears in a work that was influential in the Middle Ages, a Latin commentary, perhaps from the sixth century.[9] It maintains that the beatitudes in Matthew are spoken to those on the mountain who are perfect, to the apostles as leaders of the people, while those in Luke are addressed to the average person (Hom. 9.3). Only the disciples climb the mountain because the mountain represents the height of virtue, the peak of the church. The crowd of people who are burdened with sins or encumbered with worldly concerns may not go there to approach Christ (Hom. 21.1). Here there is a misunderstanding of the incidental observation by Matthew: "Seeing the crowds, he went up on the mountain, and when he sat down his disciples came to him" (Matt. 5:1f.). In reality, the Sermon on the Mount is aimed at everyone; the disciples represent the later church. In the thirteenth century, Bonaventure, the great Franciscan theologian, taught that Jesus was not addressing the imperfect crowds but rather the apostles on the mountain whom he wished to lead to the summit of perfection.[10] In the sixteenth century, the Spanish Jesuit Maldonatus agreed. He argued that Christ did not set forth evangelical perfection for everyone; he called the people to repentance, and to those who wished to be perfect he said, "Sell everything that you have and give it to the poor, and then come and follow me."[11]

In all likelihood this interpretation was circulated further. In fact, it can lead to a two-stage or two-story ethic, and it has often been seen simply as the Catholic interpretation. Only in the "state of perfection," namely, in assuming one's orders by adhering to the three "evangelical vows" of voluntary poverty, unmarried chastity, and absolute obedience, can the highest demands be met. But this is a false understanding of the so-called state of perfection. Thomas Aquinas says that Christian perfection is measured according to love, which all Christians must seek.[12] Assuming orders in itself does not assure perfection but only a greater opportunity to achieve perfection. Only secondarily and indirectly does the perfection of the Christian life consist of the evangelical vows, which, like the commandments, are coordinated with love.[13] The particular external "conditions" which are reflected among people in the church contribute to a certain beauty in the church.[14]

No Demands for Worldly Rulers?

In his sermons on the Sermon on the Mount in 1530–32, Martin Luther spoke against two extremes: first, the "canonists," namely, the Catholic theologians who sought to weaken the strict demands and understood them to apply in their full meaning only to monks; and second, the Anabaptists and enthusiasts who interpreted these instructions rigorously as laws and undermined the civil order by their literal exposition.[15] Indeed, the "baptist-minded" wished to take Jesus' demands seriously and thus were critical of the princes' misuse of force. In his commentary on the Sermon on the Mount, Luther defended the right of the magistrate and charged Christians to submit to him as citizens of this world. The commandment to be meek applies to the individual but not to the magistrate who bears the sword.[16] Luther tried to resolve the problem that rests in the tension between Jesus' radical demands and life in this world in his doctrine of two kingdoms: We are justified by faith and thus belong to the kingdom of God; however, in this world we must judge according to its internal laws. Today even Protestant theologians criticize Luther for giving too little consideration to an unjust earthly kingdom. But precisely in Luther's case we see how difficult it is for a Christian inflamed with the gospel to come to terms with the obligations of life in this world.

In pursuing Luther's thought, we often encounter the notion that the Sermon on the Mount with its stringent demands demonstrates one's inability to fulfill the will of God and points to the cross by means of which one will find deliverance and salvation in spite of one's own failure. Acceptance of the sinner by God's grace is, to be sure, fundamental for the doctrine of redemption as it is developed by Paul especially, but the Sermon on the Mount has a different perspective. God's mercy is assumed, but moved by it we are to act accordingly, and this activity is also possible for us. "All things are possible to the one who believes." The preacher in the Sermon on the Mount issues a vigorous summons to this action (Matt. 7:21, 24–27). That God is merciful to us, even when we fail, is another matter altogether. We must daily pray, "Forgive us our debts"; but God's constant claim, as Jesus proclaims it in the Sermon on the Mount, remains firm.

INTERPRETIVE TENDENCIES
SINCE THE ENLIGHTENMENT

The Enlightenment, that intellectual movement which penetrated all of Europe in the eighteenth century, reflects a profoundly radical change insofar as every dogmatic tie was rejected and the autonomy of human reason was lifted up. Accordingly, a religion of reason was constructed in which Jesus and his teaching also found a place. For many in the Enlightenment, Jesus was a preacher of morals, filled with strong expectations of the future, who finally died for his ideals. In the Sermon on the Mount they wanted to rediscover the law of morality which was only apprehensible by reason. A high ethos was thereby certainly developed that was to contribute to a happiness encompassing humanity. The ideals of the French Revolution had their basis in it, and the German philosopher Immanuel Kant, in his writing *On Everlasting Peace* (1795), advanced the idea of a general peace among nations. His categorical imperative, "Act only on that maxim which you can, at the same time, will to become a universal law," influenced the future, including the field of theology. But what did that mean for the interpretation of the Sermon on the Mount? Should all its radical demands be subordinated to this reasonable ethic?

Character Ethics

The liberal theologians of the early twentieth century were not at all inclined to draw radical conclusions for the shaping of public life. The Sermon on the Mount was interpreted, above all, as a character ethic. That could correctly be understood as meaning that Jesus demanded an ethic that comes from the heart and that radically alters one's way of thinking. But there is also the danger that by withdrawing into an inwardness, one shirks the consequences for practical conduct. According to Wilhelm Herrmann, Jesus wanted "to clear the way for right character." Thus he concluded, "If Jesus' words are understood from his character, they do not diminish the viewpoint that striving after power and possessions, which are protected for us by law, is morally necessary."[17] But that clearly contradicts Jesus' words.

Otto Baumgarten thinks that Jesus presupposes the validity of the unwritten laws of the world and of the economy, and that he does not want to offer a system but intensifies the entire ethic. "Above all details stands the entirely unique purity, subjectivity, sensitivity of character, that which in its deepest sense is called ethos."[18]

Such an interpretation in the early decades of our century, which in its pathos already seems strange to us, serves a cultural optimism that believes it can enrich European Christian culture in this way. But it adapts itself unambiguously to the society of the day and is blind to the serious harm it does socially. In the pathos of noble character the misery of the working class continued to decline as there were not deeds that reflected that character.

Socialistic Interpretations

Thus one need not be surprised that in other circles quite different conclusions were drawn from Jesus' ethical message. Some demanded that the social claims be translated into action and that social relationships be changed. According to Max Maurenbrecher, Jesus understood the Jewish idea of the kingdom of God in social terms; thus the most important of the collection of sayings is the beatitude regarding the poor (Luke 6:20). Maurenbrecher argues that they are promised salvation because they are poor.[19]

Of the religious socialists, one of the most impressive figures is the Swiss Leonhard Ragaz, who resigned as professor in Zurich after World War I to devote himself completely to labor among the working class and the poor. In addition to ideas about poverty, he gave much thought to the notion of peace for which he also worked publicly. His last work, which appeared in 1945, was a commentary on the Sermon on the Mount that is characterized by clarity and powerful use of language.[20] Ragaz does not manipulate Jesus' message which is based on faith in God as Lord and Father, but he emphatically sets it in our world. It is a commentary in which traces of the spirit of Jesus and of the Lord's Prayer are found on every page.

Consistent Eschatology, "Interim Ethic"

Another starting point for understanding the Sermon on the Mount is to interpret Jesus' message of the imminent kingdom of God as being consistently eschatological, that is, the "nearness" of God's kingdom announced by Jesus is shifted into the immediate future. Jesus was then mistaken about the temporal aspect; but, according to Johannes Weiss, this cannot be historically questioned. Thus for Jesus' ethic, he concludes that it is an "exceptional legislation."[21] Albert Schweitzer, who accepted the view of consistent eschatology, spoke of an "interim ethic" for the brief period prior to the coming of God's kingdom. But he tried to transfer what Jesus truly intended out of the apocalyptic way of thinking of that period into our time with a world-view that is possible for us; he came to an ethic that is powerfully demanding of us even today. Its content is an ethic of service and repentance that in essence is individualistic and world-denying.[22] Indeed, out of that Schweitzer also developed positively a heroic humanity. Well known is his phrase "reverence for life," which as a physician and as one concerned for the poorest of people, as a "jungle doctor" in Lambaréné, he for his part wanted to implement. It has been said that this is the Sermon on the Mount understood cosmically.[23]

Jewish Responses

For the believing Jew, the Torah is a divine gift that, in a significant and salutary way, shapes life in this world according to God's will and instructions. Therefore the constant objection against the radical demands of Jesus from the Jewish side is that Jesus demands the impossible and that, in contrast, the Torah is to permeate life and not destroy it by such rigorousness. Joseph Klausner writes in his book on Jesus that Jesus' demands "may be legitimate as ethical rules for the individual as the supreme form of morality. We find similar sentiments in isolated sayings of the Tannaim and Jewish thinkers of the Middle Ages. . . . But as the only legitimate standard of teaching that is sufficient for the life of the people, it could not be accepted by Judaism."[24]

In modern times, however, there are Jewish scholars who want to reclaim "Brother Jesus" (Shalom ben Chorin) completely for Judaism. Pinchas Lapide, who is well versed in the Christian discussion, has written a book, *The Sermon on the Mount: Utopia or Program for Action?* (Eng. trans. Maryknoll, N.Y.: Orbis Books, 1986). After ostensibly rejecting eight misinterpretations, he says that one must consider the two main features of Jesus' sermon: taking God with complete seriousness, which quickens in Jesus a wholesome dissatisfaction with halfway measures and compromises; and then again the realism of Jesus, who, as a profound observer of human beings, advances a radical political theology, but does so by means of practical methods that do not make excessive demands on willing persons as God's collaborators (pp. 6–7). Lapide is unable to resolve the tension between the ideal and the reality. But in the fundamental choice, he approaches the radical solution, particularly in the question of peace.

With that we are in the midst of the contemporary discussion in which Protestant and Catholic exegetes, systematic theologians and ethicists, active Christians, politicians, and many others are taking part, for whom the current issue is a burning one. We cannot consider all the voices here, but we want to examine several interpretations that are influential today.

INFLUENTIAL INTERPRETATIONS TODAY

Much from the past has had an effect on contemporary interpretations of the Sermon on the Mount, not the least being the radical resolution of a literal understanding as far as it is possible. But modern exegesis has also provided several new insights, especially in the area of Jesus' proclamation as a whole. Sketches of only a few views can be presented here that demonstrate that we are still quite far from overcoming the basic problem of how the extreme demands of Jesus are to be realized.

The first I will mention is the *existential interpretation of Rudolf Bultmann.* He presented his basic idea in his book *Jesus* (1926; Eng. trans., *Jesus and the Word*; New York: Charles Scribner's Sons, 1934). According to Bultmann, we hardly know anything certain about Jesus himself; but the kerygma, the proclamation delivered by Jesus Christ, which contains the essence of his message, requires a decision from us and demands a new human self-understanding. In terms of substance, Jesus did not demand anything in particular but rather demanded a radical obedience by means of which each person will know how to act in a given situation.

Bultmann writes, "What God's will is, is not stated by an external authority, so that the content of the command is a matter of indifference, but man is trusted and expected to see for himself what God commands. God's requirements are intrinsically intelligible. And here the idea of obedience is first radically conceived" (pp. 76–77). God's demands "arise quite simply from the crisis of decision in which man stands before God" (p. 87). "It is fundamentally a mistake to look to him for concrete ethical requirements or for his attitude toward concrete ethical problems" (pp. 88–89). Bultmann then applies this basic view to the demands of the Sermon on the Mount and interprets it as a command to do wholly and with undivided attention what is perceived to be right at the time, but not in a legalistic sense. Thus he says, "Whoever appealing to a word of Jesus refuses to dissolve an unendurable marriage, or whoever offers the other cheek to one who strikes him, *because* Jesus said so, would not understand Jesus. For he would have missed exactly the obedience which Jesus desires" (p. 92).

Here we have a pure situation ethic that undoubtedly speaks to the modern person who strives after an autonomous will to decide and that exerts a seductive attraction particularly on young people. But the elimination of material values and concrete demands is not only ethically questionable, it also contradicts the understanding of the primitive church, which took Jesus' words as instructions it was to put into concrete practice in its life, as difficult as that was in the circumstances of the times. Jesus himself, in questions posed to him, made decisions in concrete situations and took a specific position, and these directions maintain their force even in different situations. Certainly his decisions must be freshly considered in new situations, but not without regard for the contents of his statements. Thus, for example, his command to love one's enemies constantly requires an application that remains faithful to its basic intent.

Similar to Bultmann, Günther Bornkamm stresses that Jesus liberates the will of God "from its petrifaction in tables of stone"; but he sees more clearly that Jesus' call is to concrete obedience, especially in relations to one's neighbor.[25] Eduard Schweizer urges concrete action even more. To begin with, he distinguishes that part of the Sermon on the Mount which unmistakably goes back to Jesus himself, in which the cry for complete trust in the "Father" is especially clear, from other parts that are interlaced with, or superimposed by, communal interests and redactional tendencies of the evangelists. But regarding the "truth question," which may not be ignored by these voices, Schweizer gets involved in very concrete questions and behavior patterns in actual problems of our day. Jesus did not set up immediate, practical rules of conduct. What he sought was a new heart in a person that acted not out of compulsion but rather out of the freedom of faith.[26]

In his comprehensive *The Ethics of the New Testament* (Göttingen, 1982; Eng. trans., Philadelphia: Fortress Press, 1988), Wolfgang Schrage also argues that the New Testament does not insist simply on a new foundation or a change in fundamental behavior and thought but also on a Christian shape to life and a specific conduct toward the world in the individual. "The New Testament does not support a formalistic situation ethics without shape or substance, which leaves all its content up to the individual, ending all too easily in material arbitrariness or conformity to the world" (p. 10).

With regard to political activity Hans-Richard Reuter demands reason free of hatred, a gradual destruction of armaments, and a minimization of misery, force, and servitude. "It is precisely political reason that requires the freedom made possible in faith for the just and objective perception of the neighbor, a perception which—based on the actuality of the East-West conflict that concerns us—is equally distant from harmlessness and irrational fear of Communists."[27] In these and other voices, not only is a more intense awareness of the problem perceptible but also a fundamental approach to the understanding of Jesus' intention to require an activity stemming from human confidence in God: this activity surpasses normal standards and yet cannot break out of the constraints of earthly reality. But how that is possible and practicable in specific situations, how the Christian is to behave concretely in decisions that must be made, remains unclear and questionable.

Catholic Answers

Catholic exegetes today also see, more than they did before, the difficulties that result from a close, literal reading of the Sermon on the Mount. A legalistic interpretation, as if Jesus' demands were a new code of laws that would replace the earlier commandments in the Torah, is rejected. The novelty of Jesus' ethical message consists precisely in overcoming legalistic thinking and creating for ethical activity a breadth that goes beyond the law. Josef Blank would like to understand it as "ethical models" from which a statement-tendency or intention can be derived and which can, by serious reflection, carry over to the present and be facilitated by modern formulation of questions.[28] The exegete from Bamberg, Paul Hoffmann, and his colleague, Volker Eid, a moral theologian, prefer the term "ethical perspectives" in their book *Jesus von Nazareth und eine christliche Moral.* In this approach, the interpretive answer of the churches and Jesus' ethical challenge would be brought together.[29]

On the question of compulsoriness, Heinz Schürmann distinguishes the theological-eschatological appraisals and instructions from the particular ones; among the latter he understands those things which have to do with particular spheres of life and the world or particular actions. Thus one can speak of a "lasting" obligatory character only in an analogical or approximate sense, only adaptively or intentionally. Some of Jesus' words "may clearly be taken as *models of behavior* and are therefore meant paradigmatically."[30] The Catholic moral theologian Johannes Gründel maintains that compromises, in which there is a reasonable balancing of goods over against the realities in our world, are indispensable.[31]

These are all attempts to do justice to the fundamentally obligatory character of Jesus' demands without overlooking the difficulties of their application in particular historical circumstances. The moral theologians thus wish to establish moral reason as an authority, and even the exegetes must acknowledge that Jesus' eschatological message cannot be applied in particular earthly situations without the aid of expertise and reasonable moral principles.

Christians who judge spontaneously will easily regard all attempts to reach agreement as a weakening of Jesus' original intention. But throughout the centuries Christianity has experienced both sides, those who wish to weaken and appease as well as the fanatics and utopians. The insuperable Sermon on the Mount: it remains so in this brief overview of the history of interpretation, which has concentrated on the most persistent responses. Will we ever be able to understand the Sermon on the Mount? Would Jesus even want us to "understand" it?

In what follows we will want to pursue the question of what meaning the Sermon on the Mount, with its extreme demands and resonating promises, has in Jesus' proclamation. Thus we must both consider it in its two forms in Matthew and Luke and see it in the larger framework of Jesus' proclamation. It is not easy to see the transmitted words of Jesus, as they are collected in the Sermon on the Mount and articulated as a speech by Jesus in the larger context of his message, and to perceive his original intention. I hope that the Lord's Prayer will help us in this effort.

Notes

1. From press reports.

2. Frans Alt, *Frieden ist möglich: Die Politik der Bergpredigt,* Piper series, Munich-Zurich, 1983. Eng. trans., New York: Schocken Books, 1985, pp. 5–6.

3. Cf. Manfred Hättich, *Weltfrieden durch Friedfertigkeit? Eine Antwort an Franz Alt* (Munich: Olzog Verlag, 1983).

4. Leo Tolstoy, *What I Believe* (London: Oxford University Press, 1961).

5. Cf. K. Beyschlag, "Zur Geschichte der Bergpredigt in der alten Kirche," *Zeitschrift für Theologie und Kirche* 74 (1977): 291–322, esp. pp. 314–17.

6. Clement of Alexandria, *Stromata* 7.84.5; 85.1f. (Die griechischen christlichen Schriftsteller der ersten drei Jahrhunderten 17a, 60f.).

7. In Chrysostom, *Homilies on the Gospel of Saint Matthew* 16.3; 16.5; 18.4 (on love of enemies), in Nicene and Post-Nicene Fathers of the Christian Church, vol. 10.

8. *The Sayings of the Desert Fathers,* trans. Benedicta Ward et al. (Kalamazoo, Mich.: Cistercian Publications), Macarius, no. 28, p. 113.

9. *Opus imperfectum in Matthaeum* (*Patrologia graeca* 56:680–747).

10. Bonaventure, *Apologia pauperum* cap. 3, n. 8 (*Opera omnia,* 8:246). But Bonaventure also teaches that both commandments and the "evangelical orders" are based on love (ibid., n. 3 [8:243]).

11. Maldonat, *Commentarii in quatuor Evangelistas* I, ed. J. M. Raich (Mainz, 1874), p. 94.

12. Thomas Aquinas, *Summa theologiae* 2-2, q. 184, a. 1.

13. Ibid., 2-2, q. 184, a. 3.

14. Ibid., 2-2, q. 184, a. 4.

15. "Luther's Preface to the Sermon on the Mount," in *The Sermon on the Mount,* in *Luther's Works,* vol. 21, pp. 3–6.

16. Luther, *The Sermon on the Mount* at Matt. 5:5, in *Luther's Works,* vol. 21, pp. 15–25.

17. Wilhelm Herrmann, *Die sittlichen Weisungen Jesu* (Göttingen, ^{2}1907), p. 60.

18. Otto Baumgarten, *Bergpredigt und Kultur der Gegenwart* (Tübingen, 1921), p. 117.

19. Max Maurenbrecher, *Von Nazareth nach Golgatha. Untersuchungen über den weltgeschichtlichen Zusammenhang des Urchristentums* (Berlin-Schöneberg, 1909), pp. 156–58.

20. Leonhard Ragaz, *Die Bergpredigt Jesu,* Gütersloher Taschenbücher/Siebenstern 451, ^{3}1983.

21. Johannes Weiss, *Die Predigt Jesu vom Gottesreich* (Göttingen, ^{2}1900), p. 139.

22. Albert Schweitzer, *The Quest of the Historical Jesus* (New York: Macmillan Co., 1968), pp. 398–403.

23. F. W. Kantzenbach, *Die Bergpredigt: Annäherung—Wirkungsgeschichte* (Stuttgart, 1982), pp. 58–62.

24. Joseph Klausner, *Jesus of Nazareth: His Life, Times, and Teaching* (London: George Allen & Unwin, ³1947), p. 392.

25. Günther Bornkamm, *Jesus of Nazareth* (New York: Harper & Brothers, 1960), p. 105.

26. Eduard Schweizer, *Das Evangelium nach Matthäus,* Das Neue Testament Deutsch 2 (Göttingen, 1973), pp. 133f. Cf. also idem, *Die Bergpredigt* (Göttingen, 1982), pp. 110–16.

27. Hans-Richard Reuter, "Bergpredigt und politische Vernunft," in *Die Bergpredigt* (Freiburg im Breisgau, 1984), ed. Rudolf Schnackenburg, pp. 60–80, quotation p. 68.

28. Josef Blank, "Zum Problem 'ethischer Normen' im Neuen Testament," in *Herausforderung und Kritik der Moraltheologie,* ed. G. Teichtweier and W. Dreier (Würzburg, 1971), pp. 172–83, here p. 181.

29. Paul Hoffmann and Volker Eid, *Jesus von Nazareth und eine christliche Moral,* Quaest. disp. 66 (Freiburg-Basel-Vienna, 1975), pp. 23f.

30. Heinz Schürmann, "Die Frage der Verbindlichkeit der neutestamentlichen Wertungen und Weisungen," in *Prinzipien christlicher Moral,* ed. J. Ratzinger (Einsiedeln, ²1975), pp. 9–39, quotation p. 22.

31. Johannes Gründel, "Die Bergpredigt als Orientierung für unser Handeln," in Schnackenburg, *Die Bergpredigt,* pp. 81–112.

2. THE ORIGINAL MEANING OF
THE SERMON ON THE MOUNT

IF WE DO NOT WANT to take the wrong path in our interpretation of Jesus' words and their application, we must return to the question of the original meaning of the Sermon on the Mount. Otherwise we run the risk of creating an ideal according to our own criteria, of falsifying Jesus' intention, and perhaps even of misusing Jesus' statements for other purposes. The point is to grasp the essence of Jesus' proclamation and then to understand his particular sayings. Only in that way will we be able also to resolve the tensions that result from our earthly existence and our contemporary worldview.

First we must ask, Did Jesus once give such a definite speech, one that began with the Beatitudes and concluded with the parable of a house? That is quite unlikely. The brevity and arrangement of some of the sayings, the combination of various types of styles, and, above all, the method of transmission rule out the possibility of having before us a completely original sermon by Jesus. It is an early compilation of statements by Jesus that has a strong claim to be a faithful rendering of frequently expressed thoughts of Jesus. Thus we must try to proceed step by step and make use of the methods that are recognized in modern exegesis. A sound exegetical principle is that one must move from the outer form to the inner content. But that alone is not sufficient, because we cannot simply regard as a faithful rendering of Jesus' words the sayings that are gathered in Matthew and Luke—sayings that frequently vary in wording.

Proceeding from the present form of the texts, we may inquire into their prehistory in order to press toward an original form. As in archaeological excavations, we must, as it were, remove each layer to

24

reach, in the end, the bedrock, the original words of Jesus. We cannot here carry out this work in the detail to which exegetes have devoted themselves; rather, we must rely on relatively certain results.

In contrast to a widespread skepticism today that questions everything and accepts nothing anymore as a reliable Jesus tradition, we say: Many statements in the Sermon on the Mount, on which Matthew and Luke are in agreement in their transmission, bear such a distinctive stamp of originality and are so peculiarly formulated that there can be no doubt that they have their origin in Jesus. Jesus spoke to the people and to his disciples in the visual-illustrative way that is consciously pointed and inviting and, at the same time, challenging. Let us consider such easily remembered images as the splinter in one's brother's eye, and the log in one's own eye; the lamp which is not to be hidden under a bushel; the treasure in heaven which no thief can steal and moths cannot destroy; and others. The voice of Jesus resounds with refreshing originality in such sayings. But in what context did he speak these words? How does all this fit into the urgent appeal presented by the Sermon on the Mount, into an ethical program for the Christian life, and what is the relationship of this to the proclamation of Jesus as a whole?

Thus we must set the Sermon on the Mount in a larger context and try to understand Jesus' basic intention. With necessary brevity we will first inquire into the literary form of the address in Luke and Matthew, then into the history of tradition of this composition of sayings, in order to fit that ethical appeal into Jesus' proclamation as a whole and, finally, to draw conclusions for the present.

LITERARY STRUCTURE
IN LUKE AND MATTHEW

The Two Versions

If we begin with a synopsis in which the texts of the Synoptic Gospels are set beside each other, we will soon see that the "Sermon on the Mount" was transmitted in two versions: a longer one in Matthew 5—7 and a considerably shorter one in Luke 6:20–49. Because Luke observes earlier (Luke 6:17) that Jesus had come down from the mountain with only the twelve apostles he had chosen (Luke 6:13), stopped *on a level place,* and a large crowd of disciples came to him, the Lukan sermon is often called the "sermon on the plain." But it is the same address that we are used to calling the Sermon on the Mount according to the Matthean observation (Matt. 5:17). Thus Heinz Schürmann calls the Lukan address "sermon on the mountain."[1] For both evangelists it is a fundamental summary of Jesus' sermon, a manifesto, as it were, of what Jesus, as a consequence of his prophetic-eschatological message, demanded of those who believed. We may therefore characterize the Sermon on the Mount as a "programmatic address." Whether it also signifies a "program" for a new configuration of the world, we will consider later.

That this speech is in its essence the same composition of sayings in the two versions of Luke and Matthew, which we owe to the so-called sayings source (Q), can be seen in the common matrix resulting from a comparison of the two versions:

The Beatitudes	Luke 6:20–23	Matt. 5:3–12
Sayings regarding love of enemies and retaliation	Luke 6:27–36	Matt. 5:44–48; 37–42
Sayings regarding harsh judgment	Luke 6:37f; 41f	Matt. 7:1–5
The Golden Rule	Luke 6:31	Matt. 7:12
On bearing fruit	Luke 6:43–46	Matt. 7:16–21
Closing parable of the house	Luke 6:47–49	Matt. 7:24–27

If we compare this matrix with the structure of the texts in Luke and Matthew as we have them, we find that Luke offers less excessive material than Matthew. Following the four beatitudes that, along with four more, are also found in Matthew, Luke has four cries of woe that correspond precisely to the blessings and probably go back to the evangelists.

As is true for other speeches in his Gospel, Matthew expanded his Sermon on the Mount considerably in that he incorporated into this speech many statements taken from the sayings source that are found elsewhere in Luke. Included among them are the sayings about salt (Matt. 5:13), light (5:15), one's adversary in court (5:25f.), divorce (5:32), the Lord's Prayer (6:9–13); and sayings regarding collecting treasures (6:19–21), the eye (6:22f.), conflicting service (6:24), anxiety (6:25–34), answering prayer (7:7–11), the narrow gate (7:13), the "Lord, Lord" sayings (7:22f.). Beyond that, Matthew offers much material from other sources, material not found in the other Gospels; some comes from another tradition, some is the result of redactional work. It is noteworthy that Matthew thereby created new unities of meaning and gave the Sermon on the Mount a different structure. As a whole, the Lukan address may have better preserved the construction and the wording of the sayings source.

The Construction of the Lukan Address

If we read the Lukan version in its present form, we are confronted with the force of its language. In the first part (Luke 6:20–38), it is a singular call to summon up the highest forms of love and mercy for all people and to convert them into action. Out of the beatitudes for the poor, the hungry, the weeping, and the persecuted, and out of the cries of woe against the wealthy, the satisfied, the happy, and those who seek the praise of people, arises the appeal to be guided by God's mercy. It is striking that the command to love one's enemies is placed at the very beginning, in a lengthy statement that also calls for renunciation of resistance and retaliation, and for giving and lending without requiring repayment, and climaxes with the admonition, "Be merciful, even as your Father is merciful" (Luke 6:36). The sayings regarding not judging, forgiveness, and ready generosity follow immediately.

The second part is more strongly characterized by oppositions: not seeing the splinter in one's brother's eye and overlooking the log in one's own; recognizing a good tree and a bad tree by their fruit; considering a house that is built on solid ground or on sand. In the parable of the blind leading the blind (Luke 6:39), false teachers may be in mind. Finally, however, everything points to action. The parable of building a house makes a closing statement that one is not only to hear Jesus' words but also to act according to them. The whole sounds like a summons to the community of disciples to practice the new and different behavior that Jesus brings out and demands. Heinrich Kahlefeld offers his interpretation of the Lukan speech under the title *Der Jünger* (The disciple) and considers essential the notion that the conduct of the disciples must be above that of everyone else.[2] From that arise concrete consequences for the group-specific ethos of the Christian community.

The Construction of the Matthean Sermon on the Mount

The different trajectory of the Matthean Sermon on the Mount is tied together with the Jewish-Christian tradition which this evangelist assimilates, and with his circle of readers which still, or again, confronts

Judaism. This is made clear in the section Matt. 5:17–48, which first raises the question of the "fulfillment" of the law (Matt. 5:17–19) and then develops the "greater righteousness" vis-à-vis that of the Pharisees and scribes" with six so-called antitheses. For Jesus, these antitheses express authoritatively ("but I say to you") demands that supersede the law (Matt. 5:20–48). The instructions that follow concerning the works of piety (giving alms, prayer, fasting in 6:1–18), betray unambiguously a Jewish background.

But strong internal community interests also propel the evangelist. Sufficiently demonstrating this is the long speech on gathering treasures, on the one service owed to God alone, and on the urgent seeking of the kingdom of God which overcomes all anxious, earthly concerns (Matt. 6:19–34). The section Matt. 7:1–12 deepens our view of the community of disciples with diverse material. The final section (Matt. 7:13–23) reveals how much the evangelist is concerned with the danger to the community's salvation. There are corrupting intruders into the community, and in the community itself there are hollow babblers (7:21) and dangerous fanatics (7:22); but the Judge will reject them all (7:23). The concluding parable of the building of a house (7:24–27) once again calls all Christians to thought and action.

The middle section, Matt. 6:1–7:12, is difficult to understand, and the sequence of sayings there cannot be explained easily. Günther Bornkamm considers this section a "cultic didache," a fragment of teaching on the piety demanded of the Christian community. Matthew inserted the Lord's Prayer into "cultic didache" of giving alms, prayer, and fasting (Matt. 6:9–15), and in the following admonitions draws conclusions from the requests of the second part of the Lord's Prayer—conclusions that he illustrates with Jesus' sayings of admonition. Thus, to the request for daily bread he joins the sayings regarding true treasures and not being anxious; to the request for forgiveness, the warning not to judge; and to the request for deliverance from evil, the particular saying not to cast pearls before swine and the request for the certain granting of one's prayer. The Golden Rule (Matt. 7:12) then would form the conclusion of this section.[3] Whether Matthew followed this train of thought can certainly not be proven, but the observation is important that the Lord's Prayer is at the center of the Sermon on the Mount. Matthew recognized that the demands of the Sermon on the Mount must be read and understood in the light of the Lord's Prayer.

HISTORY OF TRADITION

The oldest layer of tradition that can be recognized was already evident in the common matrix in Luke and Matthew. It is the composition of the sayings source that we are able to infer only from the common tradition in Luke and Matthew. This early collection probably goes back to early preachers of the gospel, Jewish-Christian "itinerant missionaries" who, enthused by the gospel of Jesus Christ, went about in extreme frugality and poverty in order to convert Israel. This oldest matrix then certainly was incorporated early on in the churches. From the different structures in Luke and Matthew, one may conclude that the churches contributed to the continuation of the tradition, perhaps by teachers and catechists, in order to adopt the statements by Jesus in the form that was obvious and appropriate to them. A good example of this is the Lord's Prayer, whose various forms can be explained from its liturgical use in different churches. But in this process new formations arose, as we may assume, for example, in the heaping up of beatitudes in Matthew. The beatitude that is so often cited today, that of the peacemakers in Matt. 5:9, does not belong to the original text. It is for us, however, a treasured testimony from a church or an evangelist that had apprehended Jesus' intent and, in conformity with his spirit, added this beatitude which is closely associated with the command to love one's enemies.

The topmost layer available to us is the redactional stage, from which the understanding of the evangelists can most clearly be gathered. In the conception of the evangelists, the Sermon on the Mount is a manifesto for the later church and, furthermore, for everyone to whom the gospel is proclaimed.

The Beatitudes—A Starting Point for Understanding the Sermon on the Mount

If we are to group the different emphases that both evangelists created and that, in their differentiation, still allow Jesus' proclamation to be perceived, the Beatitudes offer themselves as an exemplary text. They begin the Sermon on the Mount and are, as it were, an entrance hall that captivates and sets the mood for those who enter. But how different are the mood and the expectations into which readers find themselves taken in Luke and Matthew!

In Luke 6:20–23 Jesus turns directly to his listeners and addresses the poor, the hungry, the weeping, and the persecuted. It is, in the first instance, a triad of brief beatitudes that belong together in the history of tradition:

> Blessed are you poor, for yours is the kingdom of God.
> Blessed are you that hunger now, for you shall be satisfied.
> Blessed are you that weep now, for you shall laugh.

A longer beatitude concerning the persecuted is added that might have been added later but was already in the sayings source (cf. Matt. 5:11f.):

> Blessed are you when men hate you, and when they exclude you and revile you, and cast out your name as evil on account of the Son of Man! Rejoice in that day, and leap for joy, for behold, your reward is great in heaven.

Without question, Jesus turns to the disadvantaged and oppressed groups and promises them a change in their conditions, a reversal of their present situation, namely, in the coming kingdom of God. It is a cry for salvation for everyone who groans in poverty, hunger, suffering, and persecution. It is Jesus' option for all suffering, despised, and banned individuals whom he wishes to free and redeem. This is consistent with other statements by Jesus and with his behavior as a whole. "Those who are well have no need of a physician, but those who are sick" (Mark 2:17). Jesus came to save the lost and to announce God's mercy to everyone. All of this is an expression of his messianic mission.

This view is reinforced by the cries of woe that correspond to the beatitudes:

> But woe to you that are rich, for you have received your consolation.
> Woe to you that are full now, for you shall hunger.
> Woe to you that laugh now, for you shall mourn and weep.
> Woe to you, when all men speak well of you, for so their fathers did to the false prophets.

One may assume with relative certainty that these cries of woe were shaped and added by the evangelist in order to underscore his understanding of the beatitudes. He thought of the actual earthly conditions and understood Jesus' message as God's promise that poverty, hunger, and want will one day be overcome. Out of that he also directs an urgent appeal to the wealthy and the dominant to change these conditions now. One would certainly misunderstand Luke if this were seen as a summons to economic and political revolution. *God* will change the conditions; people should only understand God's intention and do now what is possible for them. By no means did Luke intend to glorify poverty and powerlessness as such; he assumes everywhere that the poor and the oppressed will hear Jesus' message and be guided by it. It is a message of good news for the disadvantaged and those deprived of rights in the framework of Jesus' proclamation of salvation. Acceptance of the gospel is presupposed, even the gospel of nonviolence and love of enemies. The admonition, which follows immediately in Luke, to love one's enemies, to reject retaliation, to do good without expecting thanks, shows this quite clearly.

In his Sermon on the Mount, Matthew has taken up this appeal to one's own conduct, which is implied in the Beatitudes, and forcibly sets it before his communities. He presupposes the promises of God, the message of salvation, as the same or similar statements in the second part of the Beatitudes show. As if held together by a clamp, they all look toward the coming of the kingdom of God. But Matthew now shifts the accent from the promise to the challenge. His beatitudes, formulated in the third person, become a table of ethics, a religiously motivated moral appeal. The four Lukan beatitudes are recognized in the first four of Matthew's, but several characteristic additions and changes are also present:

> Blessed are the poor in spirit, for theirs is the kingdom of heaven.
> Blessed are those who mourn, for they shall be comforted.
> Blessed are those who tolerate force [the "meek"], for they shall inherit the earth.
> Blessed are those who hunger and thirst for righteousness, for they shall be satisfied.

Instead of adding woes, Matthew expands and elucidates the claim that rests in God's promise with four new beatitudes:

> Blessed are the merciful, for they shall obtain mercy.
> Blessed are the pure in heart, for they shall see God.
> Blessed are the peacemakers, for they shall be called sons of God.
> Blessed are those who are persecuted for righteousness' sake, for theirs is the kingdom of heaven.

Among these additions we find the beatitude regarding the peacemakers, which certainly is a Matthean formulation or one originating in the Matthean community but which is formulated from the spirit of Jesus, corresponding completely with his intention. Thus it must also be interpreted according to the message and conduct of Jesus. Jesus desired and demanded nonviolence, but he taught and practiced moral resistance against violence, injustice, and antisocial conditions. He required "peacemaking" in a comprehensive sense, even in the realm of society. To those who "make peace," he promises that they will be called "sons of God." If they act according to God's great example (cf. love of enemies in Matt. 5:44f.), he will also recognize them as his sons. As the following beatitude dealing with those persecuted "for righteousness' sake" (Matt. 5:10) and the additional beatitude in the form of an address (Matt. 5:11f.) suggest, a situation of persecution in the church is presupposed in which the candidates for God's kingdom had to prove themselves. That is confirmed with the Matthean formulation of loving one's enemies in which—unlike in Luke—the issue again is "persecution" (Matt. 5:44). In such extreme distress the church should demonstrate its love of the enemy.[4]

Each evangelist thus presented Jesus' message from his own perspective to the reader. Luke, who has been justifiably called the "evangelist of the poor,"[5] takes up Jesus' message in connection with Isa. 61:1f.: He came to bring good news to the poor, to proclaim release to the captives, to set free the oppressed (Luke 4:18; cf. also 7:22). Out of that, Luke rightly develops his social interest, but he understands Jesus' message in terms of Jesus' healings and acts of salvation as proclamation of the coming kingdom of God. The promises in Luke are also directed to that end, not only in the assurance that "to you belongs the kingdom of God" but also in the statements that follow in which the future liberation, brought about by God, is contrasted with the present situation.

Matthew derived his moral appeal from the same perspective. He also presupposes Jesus' promise of salvation; indeed, he develops it with traditional motifs of Jewish expectation ("be comforted," "inherit the earth," "see God," etc.). He includes no woes, but in the expansion of the beatitudes the listeners are addressed directly. Both evangelists tie together and make audible what Jesus also united in his message: announcement of the salvation offered by God, and the demand to live accordingly. What God does is always primary; everything else is derived from that. That is why the prayer that God bring in his kingdom is so urgent: it is the central petition in the Lord's Prayer. Only by trusting God are we even able to do what God demands of us; but also only when we are prepared to do what is demanded of us are we able to trust that we are participants in God's perfect kingdom.

Love of Enemy as
Jesus' Supreme Demand

At still another point we need to clarify the peculiarity of the tradition and its mooring in Jesus' proclamation. Love of enemy, which is presented by both evangelists in their respective ways as Jesus' supreme demand, cannot be denied Jesus by his word and conduct. It is certainly nothing completely new; it is not foreign to Judaism and it is not unfamiliar to the thought of non-Jewish persons. But what is unique is Jesus' grounds for it and how he proclaimed it as unrestricted conduct that knows no limits. In connection with the parable of the Good Samaritan, Joachim Jeremias writes, "This breadth of the commandment to love is without parallel in the history of the time, and to this extent, the Fourth Gospel is quite correct in making Jesus describe the commandment to love as the new commandment (John 13:34)."[6] What are the place and function of the commandment to love one's enemies in the Sermon on the Mount?

Matthew develops and explains what is demanded of the hearers of Jesus' message of salvation and of all who follow his call in the so-called antitheses, which are preceded by the programmatic statement, "For I tell you, unless your righteousness exceeds that of the scribes and Pharisees, you will never enter the kingdom of heaven" (Matt. 5:20). In these six antitheses, which are formulated over against a definite legalistic attitude in Judaism in accordance with the situation of the Matthean community, the demands of renouncing retaliation and loving one's enemies are stressed by their placement at the end. Loving one's enemies according to the conduct of God vis-à-vis all people is the supreme demand toward which everything moves. In Luke this sayings complex follows, as already mentioned, immediately after the beatitudes and woes; this supreme demand thus is provocatively placed at the beginning. Both make the same point: What Jesus proclaims as his true concern can be expressed most clearly and sharply by love of one's enemies. In Matthew it appears at the end: "You, therefore, must be perfect, as your heavenly Father is perfect" (Matt. 5:48); in Luke: "Be merciful, even as your Father is merciful" (Luke 6:36). The reference to God is unmistakable and compels one to understand the entire admonition as a religiously grounded appeal to a supreme moral effort.

In the framework of Jesus' message of the approaching and already inbreaking kingdom of God, the following must be considered: With his appearance according to God's charge, which was clear to him, Jesus now proclaims that God wishes to establish his final "kingdom" in this *kairos,* this time of the fulfillment of all prophetic promises. Now "he proves himself to be a God of such goodness and mercy that he gives himself, without setting any conditions, radically to human beings (sinners). . . . Precisely because of that, those who open themselves to the eschatological mercy of God must and can now be radically merciful themselves even in showing love for their enemies."[7] On this divine pledge, on this offer of salvation which becomes visible in Jesus' conduct and action, on this divine act of forgiveness and reconciliation rest the call and the challenge to human beings to be as merciful as God the merciful Father.

Let it be said again: If we are clear about this first, we avoid the misunderstanding that we human beings can, by our own strength, heal all human wounds, eliminate all unjust conditions, create a final state of rest, peace, and welfare. But we are called by God to follow his example and risk what appears to be humanly impossible with our trust in him. For Jesus, the issue is the crossing of all boundaries, the victory of a conduct governed by law and justice, the surpassing of all previous rules of conduct established by human beings. That is the meaning of his extreme instructions, or, as we could also say, his "radical" demands which penetrate to the roots of the human heart. He establishes them in view of God's incomprehensible conduct in spite of all earthly difficulties, detached from all otherwise human considerations and objections. It is a supreme moral appeal as a result of his union with God and his will. This must be established with all clarity and urgency before we turn to the question of how these demands by Jesus can be realized in earthly situations. First we must be gripped by Jesus' optimism which grows out of his trust in God and his salvific power: "All things are possible to the one who believes."

THE SERMON IN THE
FRAMEWORK OF JESUS' MESSAGE

If we want to grasp the meaning of the Sermon on the Mount, we must listen even more intently to Jesus' proclamation as a whole. Of course, we cannot here deal with the entire wealth of Jesus' words and deeds but must content ourselves with stressing some of the significant ones.

Exegetes today are virtually unanimous in the view that Jesus' proclamation rests on his message of God's kingdom which is both imminent and dawning. But this message is intimately interwoven with Jesus' relationship to God. This provided him the immediate certainty of his mission. Out of it grew his prophetic consciousness that now, in this time of Jesus' appearance and work, God determined definitely and finally to grant to all people his love and mercy without condition and without limit and, furthermore, to reveal and make real this love through Jesus and everything that he does in obedience to God.

So the message of the kingdom of God depends on Jesus' understanding of God; conversely, Jesus' relationship to God the Father cannot be understood without the description and proclamation of the kingdom of God. The message of the Father and the message of God's kingdom thus must be seen together. Wolfgang Schrage observes appropriately, "It is characteristic, in fact, that both come together in the preaching of the kingdom of God: the eschatological sovereignty of God is thus the sovereignty of the Father, who in his sovereignty brings forth the saving power of his love."[8] Because I will test both more closely in the Lord's Prayer, only as much as is necessary will be said here for the understanding of the Sermon on the Mount.

On Jesus' Idea of God

Throughout the Sermon on the Mount, "God" or "Father" is the foundational reference and basis of the sayings of Jesus. As we have seen, the promises in the Beatitudes presuppose God's liberating activity which Jesus promises to believing listeners. With their authoritative instructions the antitheses cannot be understood without Jesus' certainty that he was speaking in God's name. In the prohibition of swearing, Jesus appeals to the sovereignty and holiness of God: "But I say to you, Do not swear at all, either by heaven, for it is the throne of God, or by the earth, for it is his footstool, or by Jerusalem, for it is the city of the great King" (Matt. 5:34f.). Love of one's enemy is formulated and grounded in the light of the standard of God. In works of piety the statement is repeated each time: "Your Father who sees in secret will reward you" (Matt. 6:4, 6, 18). Even without the Lord's Prayer, which Matthew quotes expressly, the idea of God the Father is not absent in the Sermon on the Mount.

In two epigrammatic unities God the Father acquires an even

stronger profile: in the admonition not to be anxious (Matt. 6:25–33) and in the invitation to pray with confidence (Matt. 7:7–11). In that longer explanation in which Jesus speaks of overcoming anxious concern for food and clothing by referring to the birds of the air and the lilies of the field, we read, "Your heavenly Father knows that you need them all" (Matt. 6:32). Similarly, we are told in the instruction for prayer not to babble as the Gentiles do, "for your Father knows what you need" (Matt. 6:8).

From this statement Paul Hoffmann proceeds with a discourse on Jesus' idea of God in order to demonstrate "Jesus' simple and concrete speech about God."[9] The admonition to pray confidently falls in the same category. It almost sounds contradictory when, in spite of the assertion that the Father already knows everything that we need, Jesus now calls upon his disciples urgently to pray: "Ask, and it will be given you; seek, and you will find; knock, and it will be opened to you" (Matt. 7:7). But God wants us to ask him, even for earthly things, as the examples that follow (bread and fish) illustrate and the petition for bread in the Lord's Prayer confirms; many words are not needed, only a strong confidence. "If you then, who are evil, know how to give good gifts to your children, how much more will your Father who is in heaven give good things to those who ask him!" (Matt. 7:11). In this juxtaposition with human fathers, the "Fatherliness" of God (we might add also, God's "Motherliness") which surpasses all things comes to the fore.

Whence does Jesus have this certainty? We can say without doubt: from his own experience of God. The statements that are quoted above deal with prayer, and we do not understand them if we do not see Jesus himself in prayer. He prayed mostly while alone with his Father, apart from the disciples (cf. Mark 1:35; Luke 5:16). But the primitive church held fast to one of Jesus' prayers to his Father, the prayer in his most difficult, darkest hour, namely, when he saw his death approaching, the prayer on the Mount of Olives. "Abba, Father, all things are possible to thee; remove this cup from me; yet not what I will, but what thou wilt" (Mark 14:36). Out of this experience of God he also taught his disciples to pray and gave them the Lord's Prayer.

Only in the spirit of such a prayer is a deeper understanding of the Sermon on the Mount disclosed with its exhortations and demands. If it is dissociated from this religious foundation, it is removed to a different level, to a general human, social, or political level; one then misses the possibility of understanding it and the original intention of

Jesus. This is not to say that there are not consequences for the social, worldly conduct of disciples of Jesus: quite the contrary. But the Sermon on the Mount is misunderstood in its deep structure if one only glances at it.

On the Message of the Kingdom of God

However, Jesus' idea of God alone does not explain everything. With it is closely bound his consciousness of mission out of which he proclaims his message of the approach and present inbreaking of God's kingdom.

The announcement of God's rule is already presupposed in the Sermon on the Mount. Matthew introduces Jesus' appearance in Galilee with it (Matt. 4:17); Luke uses the "inaugural sermon" in Nazareth for it (Luke 4:16–21). But in the Sermon on the Mount itself, the reference to this message can be recognized clearly enough. The message appears in the first promise of the Beatitudes; the series of Matthean blessings is framed by this promise (Matt. 5:3, 10). The motif continues further (cf. Matt. 5:19, 20). At the conclusion of the speech that admonishes the hearers not to be anxious is the challenge, "Seek first his [God's] kingdom and his righteousness, and all these things shall be yours as well" (Matt. 6:33). Following later are the sayings about the narrow gate and the narrow way that leads to life (= to God's kingdom) (Matt. 7:13), and about entering the kingdom of heaven (Matt. 7:21). Even the closing parable about the building of a house is designed from the perspective of the coming kingdom. But above all, the Lord's Prayer, with its central request being the coming of God's rule, stands in the middle of the Matthean Sermon on the Mount.

The distinctive feature of Jesus' message is the fact that he brings to human beings God's rule of blessing as a power that is already effective now and is discernible in his word and work, and yet its perfected coming is reserved for the future. The coming kingdom of God is already announced in Jesus' salvific deeds, in his healings and driving out of demons as well as in his attention to troubled and humbled persons, his association with the despised tax collectors, and his message of good news for the poor. But all of that can be seen even more clearly in the Lord's Prayer, in which this present-future coming of God's rule is reflected. Thus we want to study it more closely in our consideration of the Lord's Prayer.

Message and Demand

The driving force behind the Sermon on the Mount is found in the inextricable connection between message and demand, and again between demand and promise. From the message of God's liberating rule arises the appeal to a corresponding behavior of human beings; and if they listen to Jesus' words, the promise is certain that they will be part of the coming kingdom. So the rule of God is a power breaking into this world that challenges human beings to a supreme effort. The Sermon on the Mount thus has the character of a warning speech based on Jesus' proclamation of salvation. It is an earthshaking summons for the life of human beings who are seized by Jesus' message.

THE SERMON ON THE MOUNT— A PROGRAM FOR A RE-FORMATION OF THE WORLD?

If we ask how Jesus' message and demand can penetrate and change today's world, we must above all keep in mind his command to love one another, and even to love one's enemies. That is a "revolution of infinite audacity and significance" (Leonhard Ragaz). The "radical" demands of Jesus, which strike at the depth of one's heart and which culminate in the command to love one's enemies, challenge all persons in their personal and social existence. The distinction between individual and social ethics is defensible only in a limited way. Ragaz observes, "One must never forget that everything the Sermon on the Mount says belongs to the truth of God's kingdom which never speaks only to one's private life, but is a comprehensible order. The instructions to the individual always have *this* background: the kingdom."[10] Paul Hoffmann writes, "The rigid distinction between private and public, religious and political, individual and social fails to recognize the indissoluble relationship of the individual with society and vice versa."[11] But that still does not address the question of how Christians are to fulfill their responsibility toward neighbor and stranger, in society and in the world.

In his book *Jesus and Community*,[12] Gerhard Lohfink writes that the Sermon on the Mount is addressed to the community of faith: at that time, the ancient people of God insofar as it accepted his message, *and* later the Christian church, which was to claim Jesus' instructions for its own domain. According to Lohfink, Jesus consciously intended his community to be a counter society, one in which the normal social standards no longer applied. The rest of society had the principles of justice, lawful order, and even necessary uses of force. But in the community of Jesus' disciples, structures of power were to be removed, legalities surmounted, one's own rights renounced, and resistance exercised against evil; indeed, love of enemy was to be made a reality.

This appears to me to be one-sided. Can Christians separate their ecclesiological and social existence in this way—especially in a pluralistic society? Can they live in two separate worlds? The church, even as a "counter society," is involved in social and political life in many ways. But there is merit in having laid out the primary reference to the faithful community in a powerful way. According to its internal structure and order, the church could and should be a model for the nonauthoritative and nonviolent society intended by Jesus, a witness for social justice, love for all people, freedom, and peace. But can the church also completely realize the demands of the Sermon on the Mount only by its own efforts?

At the end of his book *Was ist Frieden?* (What is peace?)[13] Anton Vögtle asks whether one can govern the world by the Sermon on the Mount. After careful examination his conclusion is a clear no, but he also says that the Sermon on the Mount remains a constant challenge, not only for every individual but also for leaders of nations and all peoples. The question becomes critical today particularly with regard to the issue of peace. If we want to escape the vicious circle of force and counterforce, if we want to end the wretched arms race and use the resources freed thereby to aid the suffering nations who are living at or below the minimum level for existence, then must we not act upon Jesus' command to overcome evil with good? Must we not remove the mistrust we harbor against adversaries, prepared to be the first to move toward disarmament, to renounce the production and installation of new missiles, and so forth, as Franz Alt now demands? Must we not at least introduce a process of "minimizing misery, force, and tyranny," as is supported by the Research Institute of Protestant Scholars in Heidelberg? With such demands from the Sermon on the Mount for the political arena, there will be more widely diverse points of view, even among Christians who are inspired by the same desire for peace.

The Sermon on the Mount cannot provide practical instructions for today's situation, particularly in the political realm. Also needed is a consideration of the present world situation, which is characterized by force and terror, suppression of the weak, exploitation of the poor; in short, the power of evil. Nevertheless the Sermon on the Mount remains a program, a program for every Christian, for the Christian community, and for all humanity, a program for a new world structure. This program will never be completely fulfilled in historical time, but only through the *new creation* by God. In spite of that, the Sermon on the Mount with its central theme of the kingdom of God also remains a program for historical time, a constant lesson and challenge for us.

Notes

1. Heinz Schürmann, *Das Lukasevangelium* I, Herders theologische Kommentar zum Neuen Testament, III/1, (Freiburg-Basel-Vienna, 1969), p. 320.

2. Heinrich Kahlefeld, *Der Jünger: Eine Auslegung der Rede Lk 6:20–49* (Frankfurt am Main, 1962), p. 79.

3. Günther Bornkamm, "Der Aufbau der Bergpredigt," *New Testament Studies* 24 (1978): 419–32.

4. Cf. Rudolf Schnackenburg, "Die Seligpreisung der Friedensstifter (Mt 5:9) im mattäischen Kontext," *Biblische Zeitschrift,* new series, 26 (1982): 161–78.

5. Cf. Hans Joachim Degenhardt, *Lukas—Evangelist der Armen* (Stuttgart, 1965); and Walter Schmithals, "Lukas, Evangelist der Armen," *Theologia viatorum* XII (1973/74): 153–67.

6. Joachim Jeremias, *New Testament Theology,* Part One: *The Proclamation of Jesus* (London: SCM Press, 1971), p. 213.

7. Helmut Merklein, *Die Gottesherrschaft als Handlungsprinzip: Untersuchung zur Ethik Jesu,* Forschung zur Bibel 34 (Würzburg, ²1981), p. 236.

8. Wolfgang Schrage, *The Ethics of the New Testament* (Philadelphia: Fortress Press, 1988), p. 26.

9. In Paul Hoffmann, *"Ich will euer Gott werden": Beispiele biblischen Redens von Gott* (Stuttgart, 1981), pp. 151–76.

10. Leonhard Ragaz, *Die Bergpredigt Jesu,* Gütersloher Taschenbücher/Siebenstern 451, p. 88.

11. Paul Hoffmann, "Eschatologie und Friedenshandeln in der Jesusüberlieferung," in *Eschatologie und Friedenshandeln,* Stuttgarter Bibelstudien 101 (Stuttgart, 1981), pp. 115–52; here p. 150.

12. Gerhard Lohfink, *Jesus and Community: The Social Dimension of Christian Faith* (Philadelphia: Fortress Press, 1984).

13. Anton Vögtle, *Was ist Frieden? Orientierungshilfen aus dem Neuen Testament* (Freiburg-Basel-Vienna, ²1983), pp. 109–40.

3. IMPLICATIONS OF THE SERMON ON THE MOUNT FOR CHRISTIANITY TODAY

IF WE HAVE CORRECTLY UNDERSTOOD the Sermon on the Mount, it is, for everyone, a constant challenge that repeatedly pushes us to examine our perspective and to alter our conduct. The Sermon on the Mount must not only be heard, considered, and discussed; above all, it must be translated into action. If no practical instructions for action can be immediately derived from it, it still constantly provides an impulse for us to do what is possible. We must be conscious of the narrowness of human judgment, which is dependent on various influences, and of the weakness of the human heart. So, regarding the gospel, I must try to guard against my own biases as much as possible.

If, for example, I lean toward a rejection of rearmament, I must ask myself whether the reasons for that stance, even in the interest of peace, are not stronger in today's situation. The reverse is also true: If I think rearmament is necessary, in order to assure peace by means of a balance of power, I must ask myself whether the reasons cited by the peace movement do not come closer to the spirit of the Sermon on the Mount and whether there are not other ways to come closer to peace in the world.

Or another example: If a young Christian must decide whether to enter the armed forces or to refuse for reasons of conscience, the person must reflect on the question, Is service with a weapon under the concrete conditions of the armed services, which are only supposed to secure peace, not consistent with the spirit of Jesus, who sided with the weak and spoke of giving one's life as the highest expression of love (cf. John 15:13)? Or, by declining to serve, should I make a statement for God's absolute desire for peace which is revealed in the promise of the kingdom of peace and is to be evident now? (I have always defended both possible decisions against the pressure from one or the other.) A growing understanding of the motives of other Christians who assume a different position on concrete questions is itself a contribution to peace.

If we may not separate in principle the demands in the Sermon on the Mount into individual and social, religious and political behavior, then one thing is certain: We must apply all demands *to ourselves,* incorporate them into our heart, and translate them into action wherever we are and whatever possibilities for influence we may have. We cannot call for the Sermon on the Mount to be a new program in the world without first recognizing its application to us and being moved into action. If concrete demands in particular circumstances may not be easily found and determined, there are still fixed impulses, motives for reflection and action that emerge from the Sermon on the Mount. Nothing more or less need be attempted here to see such impulses from the Sermon on the Mount for our lives as Christians today. Thus we cannot be limited to the notion of peace but rather must keep in mind Jesus' other demands. If we do not restrict "peace" simply to the external world but understand it in Jesus' sense (as well as in the rest of the Bible) as the new, comprehensive order that is created and demanded by God through his desire for reconciliation, then it is a fundamental category that also includes the other instructions for conduct that are laid out and illustrated in the Sermon on the Mount.

Not everything in the Sermon on the Mount and its implications can be discussed here. "Impulses" will be selected, which, in my opinion, affect our situation as Christians in today's world. Others may choose other emphases and find other impulses, but we are all required to become aware of such impulses, to communicate them to others, and to be mutually driven by them.

1. OVERCOMING FEAR AND ANXIETY

Of first and perhaps greatest importance today, the Sermon on the Mount can address our crippling anxiety which so easily seizes us in the light of today's problems (economic bottlenecks, unemployment, world hunger, exhaustion of energy resources, destruction of the environment, etc.) and ominous views of the future (rearmament, atomic

weapons, population explosion, reduced living space, crime, terror, to-
talitarian systems, etc.). Every demand by the preacher of the Sermon
on the Mount, as we saw, is supported and sustained by the promises
he offers to poor and oppressed persons in God's name. Confidence in
these promises can be won only if one accepts Jesus' view of God and
attains the same confidence in this God, the Father, which filled him.
It is the God who, in spite of everything that appears to suggest the
contrary, is faithful to his creation and who gives himself compassion-
ately to humanity. Without this confidence, which manifests itself in
the title of this book, Jesus' extreme demands are impossible and humanly unbearable. Without this confidence everything becomes mean-
ingless and hopeless. But can we not share with Jesus this confidence
that overcomes all anxiety and worry, learn from him, and endure even
in our time?

Here the inestimable significance of the Lord's Prayer for the Sermon on the Mount becomes evident. It is the prayer given to the disciples by their master by means of which he enables each of them to
participate in his or her own relationship with God and incorporates
them into confident prayer to the Father. In this prayer (the second
part) he expressly takes into consideration the needs, weaknesses, and
difficulties that are part of our earthly, historical existence. They are
seen realistically, and yet in the prayer they are incorporated into the
larger perspective of the coming rule of God in a way that makes possible God's victory over them and God's subjugation of them. In Part
Two of this book, which deals with the Lord's Prayer, we will pursue
this relationship between the Lord's Prayer and the Sermon on the
Mount.

Does what has been said apply only to Jesus' time, with its different world conditions and its limited perspective, when the consequences of our technological age, threatening to destroy humanity with
atomic weapons, could hardly have been foreseen? But if the future of
humanity still depends, even today, on the decisions of human beings
as they go about with these weapons—for good or evil—the view of
Jesus not only retains its significance, but it even reaches a new and elevated actuality. For without intending to engage the external affairs of
the world directly, Jesus turns to human beings with their decision-
making capability and summons them to seek and to recognize what is
truly important (cf. Matt. 6:21). Humanitarianism, understood as
comprehensive love for human beings, is at the center of Jesus' program,

but it is a humanitarianism that is to be realized by looking to God, who desires the best for human beings. God's care becomes visible for Jesus, above all, in creation, on which human beings still depend today. Without the powers of "nature," human beings cannot, even today, engage in trade and maintain a home. Even their own abilities they do not owe to themselves; rather, these abilities are freely given to them for their use.

Whenever this consciousness is awakened in individuals, they also become aware of the responsibility that is imposed on them to shape the world with their abilities. But Jesus not only awakens morality, he also becomes a prophet. He sees the limits of human ability and exceeds them in looking to God, for whom all things are possible. God has given his promise to bring creation and the human world to perfection, and he will keep it in accordance with his love and peace.

Jesus' whole message is based on this confidence. In a certain sense it is utopia, a place not to be found on any map of the earth or in any history book; yet Jesus' view is not impossible with the presupposition of faith in God. The hope that "in everything God works for good with those who love him" (Rom. 8:28) is supported by Jesus' message, which is confirmed by his destiny, the resurrection of the crucified one. Without faith that God's kingdom is imminent and has already begun, everything remains an illusion, but the Sermon on the Mount presupposes this faith and constantly gives it new impulses.

The anxiety of existence grips many people today, not the least of whom are many young people. Perhaps the lengthy admonition not to be anxious (Matt. 6:25–33) was originally aimed at the disciples who had followed Jesus in order to participate in his proclamation and life and thus had left hearth and home. In any case, it is not a call to an easy life, a withdrawal from society; rather, his disciples are to risk all their strength for God's kingdom—confident in God the Father who will then give them the necessary means to live.

In the present context it is an admonition to all Christians to value the search for God's kingdom more than wealth; it is also a warning to the rich who accumulate treasures on earth (cf. Matt. 6:19–21). Only a higher goal, a decisive and undivided service to God, that is, conforming to the central command for the well-being of humankind, provides content and meaning to human life. Even the ultimate anxiety in our "being unto death" can thereby be overcome. "And do not fear those who kill the body but cannot kill the soul; rather fear him who can destroy both soul and body in hell" (Matt. 10:28). This statement, which can be easily misunderstood (thus again, fear of God, fear of hell?), is clarified *in its intention* with the next saying: "Are not two sparrows sold for a penny? And not one of them will fall to the ground without your Father's will. But even the hairs of your head are all numbered" (Matt. 10:29f.). Again, trust in God the Father removes all fear, even the fear of death. One could add several other statements, but they would only be impulses that would suggest further study.

2. THE CHRISTIAN AND WORLDLY POSSESSIONS

As is already clear in the Beatitudes and the statements about giving alms and one's treasure in heaven—despite the Matthean coloring, clearer in Luke—Jesus was devoted to the poor in a particular way. The poverty movement of the "charismatic itinerant preachers" in the period immediately after Jesus' death certainly reflects the spirit of Jesus that had characterized his own sermon and effectiveness among the people. In recent times this option (or preference) by Jesus has been more highly regarded and employed[1] with justification in today's world situation in which poverty, particularly in the Third World, has become an alarming and explosive problem for humanity. The incredible gulf between an unsurpassable luxury, on the one hand, and a poverty sinking below the minimum for existence, on the other, has become so vast that it can go no farther without a catastrophe. What solution does Jesus offer? For he also experiences this tension in his world.

The term "alms," which is derived from Jewish piety (cf. Matt. 6:2–4) and is frequently used by Luke, can easily be misleading. In the popular mind today it often has the meaning of a small gift for beggars. Jesus' true intention is seen in the story of his encounter with the rich man, which Matthew also provides. Jesus says to him, "If you would be perfect, go, sell what you possess and give to the poor, . . . and come, follow me" (Matt. 19:21). From this man Jesus demands nothing less than the surrender of his whole fortune. Noteworthy is the motif of perfection which is found in the Sermon on the Mount (Matt. 5:48); Matthew uses the expression only in these two places. The challenge to be perfect as the heavenly Father is perfect concludes the series of antitheses and has to do particularly with love for one's enemies. So Matthew obviously considers surrender of one's possessions for the welfare of the poor to belong to those supreme demands achievable by Jesus' disciples.

The conclusions that individuals should draw from this certainly depend on their personal situation and their possibilities for action. Jesus did not call to absolute poverty all who heard his message, but the challenge remains for all to share their possessions with the poor and suffering. The good news for the poor becomes threatening news for the rich who refuse to heed this demand. "It is easier for a camel to go through the eye of a needle than for a rich man to enter the kingdom of God" (Matt. 19:24). Even that is one of those pointed, exaggerated statements which cannot be taken literally, and yet its sharpness cannot be denied. Next to striving for power, Jesus regarded wealth as the most dangerous temptation which misses the call, springing from God's offer of salvation, to a new and different kind of conduct.

If one surveys and examines all the materials in this series of questions in the Synoptic Gospels (which cannot be done here), there is little doubt that Jesus dealt with individual persons in concrete situations and demanded that they renounce earthly goods. In today's world a far-reaching question arises: Is it enough to give away a portion of one's possessions or even to surrender all of them? Must one not change the social and economic structures in order to free the countries of the Third World from their desperate situation? One must honestly say that Jesus did not directly make this demand; however, it appears to me to be a consequence of his message. Jesus could not and did not intend to overthrow the social conditions of his day as a whole or to change them fundamentally. At that time Palestine, which was integrated into the economic system of the Roman Empire, was not fertile ground for that. But with his criticism of the distribution of goods and his preference for the poor, Jesus still established clear signals that demand that we work for structural changes in today's economic conditions. All Christians must contribute to that as far as possible, especially in a democratic state.

RENUNCIATION OF FORCE, LOVE OF ENEMY, AND PEACEMAKING

In the Matthean Sermon on the Mount the beatitude of the peacemaker, the fifth antithesis regarding the renunciation of resistance, and the sixth antithesis on loving one's enemy belong closely together. In the programmatic speech in Luke those demands are bound together and placed at the beginning as the most important thing Jesus requires of his hearers. Because we have already addressed the question of peace several times, we will content ourselves here with a few observations about these texts.

No one has understood the central idea in the three examples of *renunciation of resistance* (Matt. 5:39–41) better than Paul when he writes to the Romans, "Do not be overcome by evil, but overcome evil with good" (Rom. 12:21). The three illustrations, then, are not to be understood literally as direct instruction for action. As Paul Hoffmann says, they illustrate an apparently nonsensical behavior. They employ the form of a rule that leads to a rule of conduct *ad absurdum* and thus makes possible a change in attitude. They will thereby create a chance to see the neighbor in one's enemy and to act justly toward the person as a fellow human being.[2] We can also say: With confidence in the victory of the good, even over opponents and enemies, with our greater love we shall penetrate the wall of mistrust and hatred and even move our enemies to a different behavior.

How far this is possible in the life of nations remains a question, of course, which belongs to the responsibility of politicians. We would misunderstand Jesus' intention for interpersonal relationships if we were to reject resistance in all circumstances. Wherever protection of the weak and the oppressed or the removal of unjust structures is at stake, we must be prepared to support such actions. Otherwise we would disregard Jesus' defense of the poor and the afflicted and resort to our own behavior. It is different if the point is to renounce one's own claims and to stress love which disarms the neighbor and can move toward the good. If we break through our normal behavior, something of God's new order of peace and love becomes evident, the order which he strives after with his kingdom.

On loving one's enemy, as Jesus requires it, much has been written that is valuable and stimulating. In his lengthy contribution Dieter Lührmann has examined this commandment in the light of its tradition, its mooring in Jesus' preaching, and its history in ancient Christianity. Lührmann's assertion appears to me to be crucial: In the history of tradition it becomes clear how Jesus' commandment achieves new meaning in every new situation to which it is applied. "But precisely as the word of *Jesus* it evades the actualization of the moment; it remains free and is not dissolved in its interpretation."[3]

However, that means that Jesus' command to love one's enemy, which is oriented to God's conduct and demands the most radical conduct from those who are and want to become children of God, must be heard and considered constantly anew in the specific personal and social situation. Like the love of one's neighbor, in which the will to radicality, indeed to the love of one's enemy, is already included—consider the parable of the Good Samaritan—love of one's enemy goes beyond all normal conduct and all human standards. The Golden Rule, "Whatever you wish that men would do to you, do so to them" (Matt. 7:12; Luke 6:31), serves as a guide for practical behavior just as the postscript does in the commandment to love one's neighbor, "You shall love your neighbor *as yourself.* That is not at all intended as a limitation but rather as an effective stimulus in the inner person to overcome all selfish inhibitions and to move toward action. One must place oneself in the position of the other and consider what one would then wish from one's opponent. That is, in fact, a practical rule for discovering in the present situation what is desired by the Lord.

Love knows no limits. Love of enemy is the strongest expression of the will of Jesus to overcome all barriers erected by human beings, all legal definitions, all legalism, and to enter the breadth and freedom of divine love. Therefore love, from love of one's neighbor to love of enemy, is justifiably characterized as the "supreme commandment" which is always before us, which we are always only approaching, and which we can scarcely ever completely fulfill. The apex of love is the giving of one's life for others after the example of Jesus.

TRUTHFULNESS AND FAITHFULNESS

Taken literally, the prohibition of swearing, as it is formulated in Matt. 6:33–37, seems strange to us today. Assumed is the widespread custom in Judaism for the reinforcement of a statement or a promise to call on God or even to take a vow. Various distinctions were made between vows (cf. Matt. 23:18–22); these regulations, which are somewhat subtle, are contrary to the spirit of Jesus who, in his understanding of God, rejected all human restrictions and excuses, all appeals to God. Disavowal of such conduct becomes understandable in a society for which faith in God was still an undisputed bastion, the basis for the structure of all life. Jesus shares this fundamental view, but in practice he exercises criticism from the point of view his relationship to God.

In its positive formulation, "Let your yes be yes and your no be no;

anything more than this comes from evil" (this translation unites Matt.
5:37 with James 5:12), a permanently legitimate instruction is given to
us. God is the absolute truth whose word is unconditionally reliable. If
human beings point themselves to this true and faithful God, their
words must be louder, free of falsehood and deceit, simple and direct.
Seen from a purely human point of view, truthfulness is evidence of
character and faithfulness is a fundamental feature of human social life.
But the temptation to pretense, hypocrisy, and digression from a given
promise is great. As psychologists have observed, adults wear a mask in
order "not to lose face"—and yet lose it precisely in that way. Children
are more open, at least unspoiled children, those whom Jesus loved and
about whom he said, "Unless you turn and become like children, you
will never enter the kingdom of heaven" (Matt. 18:3—however one may
more precisely interpret this statement). It is that pure, more audible
disposition which is also present in the beatitude, "Blessed are the pure
in heart, for they shall see God" (Matt. 5:8). This assertion is taken from
a so-called entrance liturgy that asks who may ascend the hill of the
Lord. Only one can do that, "he who has clean hands and a pure heart,
who does not lift up his soul to what is false, and does not swear de-
ceitfully" (Ps. 24:4). Or, in another, similar psalm: "he who walks
blamelessly, and does what is right, and speaks truth from his heart;
who does not slander with his tongue" (Ps. 15:2f.).

In Matthew's Gospel, the "hypocrisy" of the scribes and Pharisees
is frequently condemned, for they do not behave as they say or as they
would have to behave according to the true understanding of the divine
law. In John's Gospel, deception is traced back to the devil and, next to
death, is branded as hostile to the divine: "He was a murderer from the
beginning, and has nothing to do with the truth, because there is no
truth in him. When he lies, he speaks according to his own nature, for
he is a liar and the father of lies" (John 8:44). God is the most public
truth, which proves itself in Jesus' words.

Always to speak and do the truth is also, for our social situation, an
extremely hard demand that can lead in particular to no small difficulty. Do we not occasionally find ourselves in situations in which we
lie or at least conceal the truth in order to protect and defend others?
But before all such intricacies, on which the moral theologians rightly
reflect in determining the values worth preserving, stands Jesus' call to
absolute truth and faithfulness in view of the holy and true God. That
is a gauge of our relationship to God and, at the same time, a force

toward true humanity. "God provides the strength to obey the truth" (Leonhard Ragaz).

SEXUALITY AND MARRIAGE

Two antitheses in Matthew also deal with sexual desire and marital faithfulness. They are formulated just as radically as the other antitheses, such as refusal to resist and love of one's enemy. In today's customary thought and conduct they are especially offensive. One often hears: No one has the right to lecture me in this regard, neither parents nor the church; it is my own personal concern. But Jesus, who presents us with the holy will of God the Creator and Lord, lectures us, and in a very vigorous way: "Every one who looks at a woman lustfully has already committed adultery with her in his heart" (Matt. 5:28). Jesus seizes the inner heart of human beings in a radical way so that there is no excuse. It is noteworthy that he speaks of the adultery of the man, although in the view of the time the woman was seen most frequently as the guilty party. In God's name Jesus takes a positive stand for the dignity of the woman and stresses the man's responsibility before God.

The prohibition of divorce follows the same course. The commandment of Moses is even expressly juxtaposed to it, in which the woman against whom something shameful is found must be presented with a certificate of divorce. At that time, this had led to a relaxed practice of divorce, and those who suffered were again the women. Jesus intervenes here in the name of God and forbids any divorce at all. Divorce is adultery and opposed to the will of God. What Jesus demands is absolute faithfulness to that which God desires in the marital bond between husband and wife.

With regard to the moral obligation, which cannot be captured in legal regulations, Rudolf Pesch speaks of "free faithfulness."[4] However, one may not misinterpret "free faithfulness" as whatever pleases; rather, one must understand it as faithfulness to the union entered into before God in human freedom, the supreme commitment to one's partner. The Protestant author Ragaz does not hesitate to say, "For that reason marriage is a sacrament, and only as such is it true marriage. Thus marriage is also something *exclusive*. Monogamy is the demand of the one Lord."[5] We should seriously consider these statements by a man who with all determination stands up for the just distribution of goods and the issue of peace in the world. One cannot be radical in the one question and then relativize everything in another—here, the marriage partnership.

The prohibition of divorce, which the primitive church wanted to enforce in its strict sense (cf. Mark 10:11f.; 1 Cor 7:10), posed many difficulties for the early Christian communities. In specific cases concerned with how they should live in the world (for example, if a non-Christian marriage partner wanted to separate or had already separated), practical solutions had to be sought. We cannot deal with the still more pressing problematic of today. However, we also may not disregard the urgent call of Jesus in this question. What remains as a constant reminder is the demand of responsibility for one's partner and of absolute faithfulness. As God does not go back on his promise, human beings may not do so either. Even in the realm of sexuality and marriage God establishes his liberating kingdom; people do not become truly free when they pursue their own appetites. Trusting in God the Father, human beings, even in the face of their most powerful instincts, are capable of more than they wish to admit. Even the grace of celibacy, in order wholly to serve the kingdom of God, can be given to them (cf. Matt. 19:11f.).

IN THE COMMUNITY
OF BROTHERS AND SISTERS

In the Matthean Sermon on the Mount the community from whose tradition it arises and for which it is written can be seen everywhere. Originally, it must have been composed predominantly of Jewish Christians who still preserved much of the Jewish milieu. This community took over the title of brother from Judaism but heightened it in Jesus' sense. Goodness and reconciliation are more than worship and sacrifice (cf. Matt. 5:23f.). In general, the notion of the brotherly community penetrated these Christians deeply. One of the most important assumptions for this is mutual understanding and forgiveness (Matt. 7:3–5; Luke 6:41f.).

The admonition "Judge not, that you be not judged. For with the judgment you pronounce you will be judged" leads one inexorably to look to God, the Lord and Father of all. In his interpretation of this program Ragaz asks, Are we not to call the good good and evil evil? For the sake of love are we to disavow the truth and for the sake of peace avoid conflict? No, he answers, for that reflects dishonest pacifism and neutrality with great harm to the realm of truth as well as to love and peace. "The judgment that Jesus means is the judgment of persons against persons in the sense of a tendency to condemnation, indeed damnation, which is linked to the self-righteousness which judges oneself. Empirically, this judgment is a cancerous evil in all religion, piety, and church loyalty."[6]

We will understand this better if we make it clear that in condemnation lies hidden a desire to control others. Service, not control, however, is the basic law for the community of disciples which Jesus expressed elsewhere: "Whoever would be great among you must be your servant" (Matt. 20:26f. par.). In the warning speech against the scribes and Pharisees is the statement, "You have one teacher, and you are all brethren" (Matt. 23:8). With that, all power structures, as they are to be found in the world, are rejected by the community of disciples. The Christian community has only one Lord and Master, who guides it with his word, his love, and his mercy: Jesus, who made himself on earth the servant of all (cf. Luke 22:27; John 13:4–7), gave his life as a ransom for many (Matt. 20:28), and from heaven he will lead his church in the same spirit (cf. Matt. 28:20).

Here the church achieves its special significance as an authority-free zone, as a society that contrasts with the ambition and desire for power that governs the rest of society (Gerhard Lohfink). Such a society of sisters and brothers in which everyone could find happiness and security would be a constant irritation for states and nations in which there is a crass opposition between poor and rich, high and low, and where hostility between classes and races prevails. But we all know how far we are in our Christian churches from that ideal presented by Jesus. Thus Jesus' call to a community of brothers and sisters applies especially to the community of disciples and to the later church that grew out of it.

Whoever has grasped the spirit of brotherhood will strive to embody it everywhere, not simply in church groups but also in encounters with all people, especially foreigners and persons of a different skin color and culture. Brotherhood must be practiced every day. Christ himself, the Master, became brother to all of us.

PRAYER AND SPIRITUALITY

A final word on religious life in a narrower sense. In the Matthean Sermon on the Mount the part on almsgiving, prayer, and fasting (Matt. 6:1–18) is a pictorial lesson on how a person is to stand before God and behave toward him. The crucial factor is evident in all three examples: you are not to seek reward and honor among people, but rather, your Father, who sees in secret, will reward you (vv. 4, 6, 18).

An immediate relationship to God which the individual seeks to exercise in doing good, praying, and self-denial is not very important to many people today. There are even theologians who defend Christianity without religion, that is, without any conscious relationship to God and exercise of piety. But that was not Jesus' view. He adapted himself to the religious life of his people even if he also, like the prophets, criticized a superficial cult. He himself was one who engaged much in prayer, who liked to withdraw alone, consider his life before God, and then return to fresh activity with people. That is how we also understand the command to pray in solitude and without many words (Matt. 6:6).

Private prayer does not exclude common prayer. The Lord's Prayer is formulated in the "we" style and was used in the liturgy in the worship of communities. Heinz Schürmann believes it was first intended as a prayer for each disciple, perhaps even with one reciting the petitions and wishes and the others responding with a formula of praise. But, as the we form indicates, the individual must always understand that he or she is to pray in community with brothers and sisters. The Father to whom the prayer is directed is the Father of everyone.[7]

If in recent years a tendency toward meditation has again been awakened, and young people, in particular, demand from the faith reflection on and meaning in their lives, that is fully in keeping with the spirit of the Sermon on the Mount. As we have seen, its promises and demands can only be understood from Jesus' religious perspective. The more we immerse ourselves in it, the more the profound meaning of the Sermon on the Mount will become part of us. We will never completely master it, as if we could wholly fulfill its demands; but borne by trust in the Father and faith in the dawning of God's kingdom, we will be able to internalize it and approach its goal. If we reflect on the Sermon on the Mount in the spirit of the Lord's Prayer constantly in fresh ways and apply it to our own situation, it will encourage us and help us understand our human existence, discover community with other persons, and endure the difficult struggles we face in the world.

In this struggle we do not stand alone but are bound together with like-minded sisters and brothers. Only in common effort is it possible to come closer to the goal of God's kingdom which Jesus established. Even if the full kingdom of God can and will be brought about only by God himself, still in this world that vision can be realized which Matthew presents to the community of disciples immediately following the Beatitudes: "You are the salt of the earth; but if salt has lost its taste, how shall its saltness be restored? . . . You are the light of the world. A city set on a hill cannot be hid. Nor do men light a lamp and put it under a bushel, but on a stand, and it gives light to all in the house" (Matt. 5:13–15). It is a vision that gives us hope and leads to fresh activity.

Notes

1. Cf. Luise Schottroff and Wolfgang Stegemann, *Jesus and the Hope of the Poor* (Maryknoll, N.Y.: Orbis Books, 1986); and Wolfgang Stegemann, *The Gospel and the Poor* (Philadelphia: Fortress Press, 1984).

2. Paul Hoffmann, *Eschatologie und Friedenshandeln,* Stuttgarter Bibelstudien 101 (Stuttgart, 1981), pp. 133f.

3. Dieter Lührmann, "Liebet eure Feinde (Lk 6:27–36/Mt 5:39–48)," *Zeitschrift für Theologie und Kirche* 69 (1972): pp. 412–38; here 438.

4. Rudolf Pesch, *Freie Treue: Die Christen und die Ehescheidung* (Freiburg-Basel-Vienna, 1971).

5. Leonhard Ragaz, *Die Bergpredigt Jesu,* Gütersloher Taschenbücher/Siebenstern 451 (1983), p. 59.

6. Ibid., pp. 151f.

7. Heinz Schürmann, *Das Gebet des Herrn* (Freiburg im Breisgau, ⁴1981), pp. 132f.

PART 2. THE LORD'S PRAYER

THE LORD'S PRAYER

IN HIS WORK *On Prayer* (ca. 200), Tertullian calls the Lord's Prayer a *breviarium totius evangelii,* a "brief summary of the whole gospel."[1] That is so simply because the idea of God and the message of God's kingdom by which Jesus' proclamation is conveyed immediately seizes the worshipers; but the second part of the Lord's Prayer, which contains petitions for our earthly-historical existence, also belongs inseparably to that in which Jesus was engaged in his encounters with people, in his words and actions. Precisely for that reason we now turn from the Sermon on the Mount to the Lord's Prayer, for it can lead us to a deeper understanding of that penetrating programmatic address.

At the World Mission Conference in Melbourne, Australia, in 1980 (at which I was permitted to participate as a Catholic observer) the message of God's kingdom in our world came up for discussion and was considered in the context of the petition in the Lord's Prayer, "Thy kingdom come." The pertinent question was that of the proclamation and the realization of this message in our time, particularly in Third World countries. The often excited discussions over the tensions in North-South incomes, between rich and poor nations, as well as over the issues of Christian evangelization and Christian activity in disadvantaged and oppressed countries, were accompanied by discussions of the Lord's Prayer. In these groups in which church leaders and theologians of the Western world sat together with representatives of developing countries, including many active Christians, the problematic and dynamic of the Lord's Prayer became evident to me as nowhere else before. Whenever the theologians focused attention on the future of God's kingdom, promised and established by God, the representatives of those tested and plagued persons of the Third World always asked what that means in the present and what we would have to do so that God's liberating rule would become tangible and visible. The tension between promise and reality, between pledge and demand, often escalated to passionate appeals. Final resolutions were nowhere visible; however, the prayer of our Lord led the disputing minds together, and in common prayer and singing something of the peace of God still descended on those assembled.

Countless times this "prayer of the Lord" has been prayed by countless persons over the centuries. It has been prayed in all possible languages and dialects, first in Jesus' native tongue, Aramaic, then in Greek, as it has been passed on to us, in Latin, Syriac, Coptic, Ethiopic, and others, then also in more modern languages and dialects of Africa, South America, Asia, and the South Sea Islands. In the Paternoster church on the Mount of Olives in Jerusalem it is written on the walls in many translations.

The Lord's Prayer has also been prayed in a wide variety of ways, by silent worshipers "in closets," by churches in worship, by individual groups in their particular circumstances. Sometimes it has been recited like an uninterrupted prayer chain, like musical accompaniment, almost as if it were a magical formula or a mystical oath similar to the Buddhist *om mani padme hum* ("O jewel in the lotus"). That was certainly not the intention of Jesus, who says in Matthew, "Do not heap up empty phrases as the Gentiles do."

If this was a real danger for a long time in Catholic circles, deliberation has ensued in recent years. Vatican II created a change in its reform of the liturgy. Now we pray or sing it slowly at the culmination of the celebration of the Eucharist, as the great table prayer of the church. Privately, we no longer use it like an old coin; rather, we pray it thoughtfully, contemplatively, trying to make ourselves conform to it wholly and to internalize it. We also pray it with Christians of different confessions, in the ecumenical version that was arrived at only with great difficulty. We can even pray it together with believing Jews, with whom we have much in common in this prayer.

The Lord's Prayer has repeatedly received scholarly attention in our century. German scholars such as Gustav Dalman, Paul Fiebig, Ernst Lohmeyer, Karl-Georg Kuhn, Joachim Jeremias, and Catholic biblical scholars such as Anton Vögtle and Heinz Schürmann have dealt assiduously with the origin and structure and with the contents and meaning of the Lord's Prayer. Foreign, especially Anglo-Saxon, researchers have also taken part. The most comprehensive work is by a French scholar, Abbé Jean Carmignac, *Recherches sur le "Notre Père."*[2] Meditation literature on the Lord's Prayer is abundant. Several years ago the senior editor at the Herder Publishing House, Dr. Theophil Herder-Dorneich, established a foundation, Oratio Dominica, built a chapel for it, and published much literature. A compilation of the literature alone comprised an entire book. We cannot go into all of it here; however, recognizing our debt to the research, we return to the original source texts in Matthew and Luke.

If we are to approach the original meaning, namely, Jesus' intention, we must—as with the Sermon on the Mount—begin again with the external form: the two texts we have in Luke and Matthew. Then we must study the content and construction of these texts, also comparing them to ancient Jewish prayers with which the Lord's Prayer has several important elements in common. But then we must inquire into the peculiarity and uniqueness of the Lord's Prayer, which must tie together with Jesus' proclamation. If we also come upon Jesus' relationship to God and to his message of God's rule, we will more deeply grasp the meaning of the prayer. In the light of the Sermon on the Mount, the second part of the prayer, with its petitions for our earthly-historical existence, merits special attention not only because of its grappling with the great concern in the prayer that God's kingdom come but also because these petitions are not far removed from the texts of the Sermon on the Mount and cast new light on its demands.

Notes

1. Tertullian, *De oratione* 1.6 (Corp. Christ., Tertulliani opera I, p. 258).
2. Jean Carmignac, *Recherches sur le "Notre Père"* (Paris: Ed. Letouzey & Ané), 1969), 608 pages.

4. THE UNMISTAKABLE PRAYER OF JESUS

THE TWOFOLD TRADITION IN LUKE AND MATTHEW

As was the case with the Sermon on the Mount, the Lord's Prayer comes to us in a double tradition in Luke and Matthew. As with the Sermon, a briefer text is found in Luke (Luke 11:2–4) and a lengthier one in Matthew (Matt. 6:9–13), the latter having become part of our practice of prayer. However, in contrast to the Sermon on the Mount, which for both evangelists takes approximately the same place in portraying the work of Jesus, the prayer of the Lord is placed in different contexts. In Matthew it is in the Sermon on the Mount; in Luke it is in the great interpolation he shaped which, according to its external framework, is also called the "travel report" (Luke 9:51–18:14 or 19:27). These different arrangements are noteworthy and instructive in terms of the intention of the evangelists and the background of the tradition.

The Setting of the Two Sections

In the travel report, which in nine to ten long chapters describes Jesus' journey from Galilee to Jerusalem, Luke compiled much traditional material that is not found in Mark (hence "interpolation" into the Markan portrayal). This material is created by Luke in part out of the sayings source and in part out of other sources (Luke's "special material"). On this "journey" which depicts only an artificial milieu, Jesus encounters many persons, teaches the disciples, heals people, engages in conversations, tells parables, gives advice, and so forth, in lively succession.

Luke, the great collector, has brought together here under his own direction much that he found in traditions and considered important for his readers. If one surveys this rich material, certain narrative complexes and aphoristic units are noticeable that the evangelist obviously wanted to arrange thematically. After the sending out of the disciples (Luke 10:1–24), three segments follow that are to provide a fundamental orientation for living the Christian life: the love command with the example of the parable of the Good Samaritan (Luke 10:25–37) which calls love to action; the scene with Mary and Martha, who ardently listen to and consider Jesus' words (Luke 10:38–42); and finally a longer section on prayer (Luke 11:1–13). This appears to be something of a catechism of the primitive Christian church that immediately introduces one to the fulfilled Christian life. Engaging in acts of love, based on the word of God as Jesus proclaimed it, and meditating and praying in the spirit of Jesus are essential elements of the Christian life.

The section on prayer in Luke 11:1–13 contains three parts of Jesus' instruction on prayer: in the first position is the Lord's Prayer (Luke 11:2–4), then the parable of the importunate friend (Luke 11:5–8) which perhaps should more appropriately be called the parable of the listening friend, and finally the sayings on confident prayer (Luke 11:9–13), which Matthew also includes in the Sermon on the Mount (Matt. 7:7–11). For this instruction on prayer which was collected from the Jesus tradition, Luke, who is also justifiably characterized as the "evangelist of prayer," created a special introduction. Frequently he says that Jesus lingered in prayer (Luke 3:21; 5:16; 6:12; 9:18, 28f.), and he begins that way also here: "Jesus was praying in a certain place," and then he continues, "and when he ceased, one of his disciples said to him, 'Lord, teach us to pray, as John taught his disciples'" (Luke 11:1). We know nothing about the prayer of John's disciples; but Luke's introduction presupposes the awareness of the later Christian church that it owes the Lord's Prayer to Jesus himself. It is the prayer that the Lord taught his disciples. Jesus then expressly says, "When you pray, say," and the Lord's Prayer follows in its Lukan form (Luke 11:2).

In Matthew the Lord's Prayer is introduced quite similarly: "Pray then like this" (Matt. 6:9); but, as we saw, it is inserted in the instructions on the Jewish practice of piety and also has wording that is varied by Luke. How important it was to Matthew is seen in the comparison with prayer for show as practiced by Jews (although certainly not the rule) and with the "babbling" of the Gentiles; it holds a very central place in the Sermon on the Mount and is recognizable also here as a prayer taught by Jesus himself.

Sitz im Leben

Thus we come to the "setting in life" of the respective traditions. Luke, who writes for Gentile Christian readers, wanted to teach the young Christians coming out of paganism how to pray and to do so in the way Jesus prayed, that is, to pray in the spirit of Jesus. The most important aspect for him in the three parts of his instruction on prayer was confidence in God the Father. This concern lies behind the two other texts besides the Lord's Prayer. The point of the parable of the importunate friend is that if a man who wants to help a friend in need shrinks from no effort to fulfill his friend's request, perhaps even out of an inferior motive not to be ashamed, or on account of his importunity (the Greek expression can mean both), God will all the more certainly hear the requests of those who call upon him for help (cf. also the parable of the unjust judge, Luke 18:1–7). The group of sayings on confident prayer point in the same direction: If a human father gives good gifts to his son when the latter asks him, how much sooner will God give good things (in Luke: the Holy Spirit) to those who ask him!

Matthew comes out of the Jewish-Christian tradition and writes particularly for Christians who grew up in Jewish piety. His emphasis is somewhat different: no long, wordy prayer, because the Father knows what the person in prayer needs before he or she even turns to God (Matt. 6:8). It is also true for Matthew that prayer bears fruit for the life of the community. Thus, at the end he adds another admonition that takes up the request for forgiveness: "For if you forgive men their trespasses, your heavenly Father also will forgive you; but if you do not forgive men their trespasses, neither will your Father forgive your trespasses" (Matt. 6:14f.). That is a matter which the evangelist also pursues in the parable of the unforgiving servant (Matt. 18:23–35). Both evangelists, therefore, tailored their instructions on prayer to their circle of readers.

But with that we have not yet described the actual *Sitz im Leben*. Both evangelists came upon the Lord's Prayer and only inserted it into their respective contexts. Where did they come upon it? Surely in the liturgical and prayer life of their communities. That also explains their different wording of the text. The excessive language, which we noted in the Matthean Lord's Prayer and about which more will be said, betrays Jewish thought and Jewish language. Luke elucidates the picture of debtors for his Gentile readers with the forgiveness of sins and also formulates differently the petition for bread. But the original wording and the meaning of the Lord's Prayer are affected very little.

The varying forms of the text provide a hint of the original text, which was merely adapted for use in communities that were differently constituted. There can be no doubt of the recitation of the Lord's Prayer in primitive Christian communities. In their worship, but also in private prayer, the prayer of the Lord had a fixed place, as a little later the *The Teaching of the Twelve Apostles* also attests (8.2), where it is added, "You should pray three times a day" (8.3).

If the Lord's Prayer entered the practice of primitive Christian communities in this way, there can hardly be any other explanation than that from the very beginning it was believed to be the specific prayer that Jesus taught and passed on to his disciples. Thus, in the Lord's Prayer we come upon the original statement by Jesus that proceeded entirely from his spirit and intention. For us that is what makes the Lord's Prayer so special: In it the thoughts of Jesus are tightly collected, in it we have a "key to understanding Jesus" (Heinz Schürmann).

The Original Form

If we consider the additions and changes by the evangelists or their traditions, we may come closer to the original form of the Lord's Prayer. In Matthew the following phrases are recognizable as additions (in the Jewish-Christian mind):

> the expanded address "who art in heaven"
> the petition "Thy will be done on earth as it is in heaven"
> the second part of the petition not to be led into temptation: "but deliver us from evil"

Characteristic for Jesus is precisely the immediate, trustingly familiar address of God with "Father," as will be shown. The Lukan brief address "Father" is certainly the original. Out of respect for God the Jews go to great pains to guard God's grandeur, and Matthew also feels obliged by this reverential speech. With all "confidence" in God it can by no means now be overlooked that the "Father" also remains for Jesus the "Lord of heaven and earth" (cf. Matt. 11:25/Luke 10:21), but not in that distance and removal from the world which makes access to him for human beings difficult and makes him more of a lawgiver and judge. Jesus wants to bring us closer to this God in his grace and mercy.

The petition that God's will be done is a development of the great prayerful wish that his kingdom come. Thus, it offers nothing fundamentally new vis-à-vis this comprehensive request, but elucidates it. Heaven and earth are juxtaposed: As God's will is already a reality in the heavenly realm (in the world of angels), it is also to be accomplished on earth. That gives God's kingdom, as an event to be realized on earth, a powerful force; but there remains a petition to God. God himself is to make the future fulfilled kingdom increasingly visible and evident in this world.[1] Indeed, God's will also thus becomes a demand on human beings (cf. Matt. 7:21; 12:50; 21:31), just as the petitions to the Father that follow do not exclude human efforts but rather call them forth. But God's salvific work is the first thing that makes all human effort possible, and that is the meaning of this particular petition.

If God is to deliver us from evil, that is tied closely to the preceding clause as an elucidation ("but"). The "temptation" into which God is not to have us slip is one behind which the power of evil stands. If a person is exposed to such a salvation-threatening danger, that person is too weak to withstand it on his or her own: the appendix which forms a new petition is intended to express this. As it was for the Matthean community, this petition is also to help us understand "temptation"; however, it may not belong to the original body of the Lord's Prayer. If the two remaining prayer wishes or petitions had been known to Luke, he would hardly have omitted them.

The shorter Lukan version of the Lord's Prayer is completely contained in the Matthean text. The five petitions form the basic content of the prayer that Jesus taught his disciples, and they indicate that we are moving closer to the original text. Only the clarifying formulation "Forgive us our sins" (instead of "debts") might go back to Luke or his prototype. If we consider the continuation of "every debtor," whom we also are to forgive, the original wording is betrayed, that of the forgiveness of "debts."

It is difficult to answer the question how the bread petition originally read. Neither the Matthean "give us this day" nor the Lukan "daily" can unequivocally claim precedence. That is because of the difficult adjective accompanying "bread," which we can only consider in the explanation (in chap. 6). The meaning is hardly altered by this uncertainty; we are still able to see Jesus' intent.

Some exegetes believe that the second part of the petition for forgiveness, "as we forgive our debtors," which violates the style of petitions, is not original,[2] and thus not added by Jesus. It is possible that the worshiping community added it early on because it corresponds to Jesus' demand that we forgive our brother again and again (cf. Matt. 18:22 and the adjoining parable of the unforgiving servant). But because that was so close to Jesus' heart, the assurance could also originate with him—must we require a strictly proper style and form of the Lord's Prayer? Be that as it may, the addition was already present in the Q source, as the corresponding tradition in Matthew and Luke attests.

The concluding doxology (For thine is the kingdom and the power and the glory forever. Amen) is absent in the oldest manuscripts and is not uniformly rendered by later ones. It is certainly not part of the original form, although Joachim Jeremias believes that a closing doxology belongs to such a prayer.[3] But even its absence can be seen as significant as to Jesus' intention in this prayer. It "corresponds to the observation that it opens without a doxology." The Lord's Prayer seems "to end with a cry for help which in its distressful urgency would rise above all liturgical concluding celebration," writes Heinz Schürmann.[4]

Thus from the received texts emerges an extremely brief yet very pregnant prayer that we may view with great certainty as the prayer Jesus gave his disciples.

STRUCTURE AND CONTENT
OF THE LORD'S PRAYER

The earlier beloved and widely disseminated version of the "seven petitions," which (at least in the Matthean form) appears not to be unwarranted, needs scrutiny and correction. In particular one must distinguish the petitions in the first part (Hallowed be thy name, thy kingdom come), along with the elucidation in Matthew (Thy will be done on earth as it is in heaven), from the actual petitions on our behalf in the second part. Externally recognizable is the distinction between the you formulations in the first part and the we formulations in the second. Moreover, the opening petitions have a different linguistic form: first the verb, then the subject; they stand unconnected next to each other, although internally they belong close together. The petitions place an imperative together with an object and also use "and" as a connective (in the second and third petitions). This two-part structure of the Lord's Prayer is essential for its understanding.

The only meaningful internal structure looks like this:[5]

Address
The first three petitions:
   Opening petition: Hallowed be thy name.
   The great petition: Thy kingdom come.
   The Matthean elucidation: Thy will be done on earth as it is in
      heaven.
The last three petitions:
   Give us this day the bread necessary for today,
   and forgive us our debts as we forgive our debtors,
   and lead us not into temptation, but deliver us from evil.

The petitions in the first part take up Jesus' proclamation and present it in prayer and praise before the Father because only he is able to bring the announced rule of God to its final fulfillment. However, for the time in which we live, between the dawn and the consummation of God's kingdom, the most important concerns are formulated as petitions to the Father.

In these petitions human existence is understood in all its dimensions. The petition for bread refers to our earthly dependence on food. The petition for forgiveness goes deeper: It sees our spiritual-personal existence threatened by sin and guilt. The petition that God not lead us into temptation, which is related to the petition for forgiveness, is also aimed at the future and thus includes our whole historical being.

If the three petitions are taken together, an understanding of humanity lies behind them that becomes clear from the statements and instructions of Jesus. Human beings are seen in their earthly-historical existence, but at the same time in their place before God, in their spiritual-personal being which lifts them above the rest of creation. In their juxtaposition to God their life is fulfilled, in their responsibility before God they must carry out their duties, and in their relationship with God their whole existence becomes meaningful and sound.

Both parts of the Lord's Prayer are related to each other. Without God's fulfilling work our life remains under the influence of earthly needs and perils to our salvation and, finally, is without hope. Yet God's coming kingdom is no distant dream or consolation; rather, it breaks into our time if we implore the Father and follow the call of Jesus. It is a prayer and, therefore, God stands in the forefront with his work and activity; but our human response and our efforts to conform to his will are included in it. Thus the Lord's Prayer is central to Jesus' thought and a focal point of the challenge to his disciples.

This content of the Lord's Prayer, which can only be outlined here, will be developed later. Further questions are raised with the delivery of this prayer to the disciples. Is the Lord's Prayer a formula for prayer or instructions for prayer, that is, only a pattern for the way in which the disciples are supposed to pray? The tight form in which it is presented shows that it is to be a model prayer that is to be recited in its brevity. But the two forms in which it has come to us also show that the early communities did not feel slavishly bound to the wording. The prayer of the Lord is also "open" to clarifying additions, to a "prayerful unfolding" (Heinz Schürmann).

Who are the addressees? Is this prayer delivered to the narrower circle of disciples as a distinguishing mark, as it were, vis-à-vis other groups in Judaism at the time, as is suggested in Luke's introduction? That is certainly true, but not to the extent that Jesus intended to establish thereby a separate community. His message remained open to everyone who wanted to hear and follow his message, which was aimed at the entire nation. After Easter it became the common prayer of all disciples of Christ, and its petitions can still move strangers.

COMPARISON WITH JEWISH PRAYERS

At this point where the uniqueness of the prayer that Jesus gave his disciples is clear, its roots in the Old Testament and its similarity to Jewish prayers must be considered. Jesus' message cannot be understood without its prehistory in the thought of his people, his appearance being aimed at winning the ancient people of salvation for his proclamation. Thus we must also consider the lines that connect the Lord's Prayer to the rich prayer life of the Jews.

In his instructive contribution Alfons Deissler exposes its roots in the Old Testament.[6] The genre of the Lord's Prayer can be seen in the similar structure of prayers in the Old Testament: It is always a matter of the way and rule of God in history and of the way of human beings. Similar prayer petitions can be detected in the rich Jewish prayer literature for the particular texts of the Lord's Prayer. For the most part they are longer prayers in which the great concerns of Israel as well as personal needs are addressed. The Kaddish prayer, which was developed from early statements into a much-used way of praying in Jewish worship, stands particularly close to the Lord's Prayer. Most well known is the so-called Kaddish of the "orphans or mourners." The agreement with the Lord's Prayer in the first two great petitions is especially noteworthy:

> May his great name be exalted and hallowed in the world which he created according to his will. And may he bring his kingdom to rule in your life and in your days and in the life of the whole house of Israel quickly and soon, and you shall say, Amen!

In the second part, further praise of God's name follows, and then:

> May your prayer be heard and your petitions be answered with the petitions of the whole house of Israel before our Father in heaven. May heaven bring great peace, help, deliverance, release . . . for the whole community of the whole house of Israel for life and peace, and you shall say, Amen!

Thus, in the Kaddish we find Jesus' central petition: "Thy kingdom come," and also the subsequent designation of God as "Father in heaven." Of course, differences with the Lord's Prayer are not to be overlooked: Not to be found in the Kaddish is the entire second part with its petitions for earthly needs and dangers, as well as the connection between the petitions in the first part and the threats to our human and historical existence which is so characteristic of the Lord's Prayer. In this Jewish prayer attention is directed particularly at the "life of the whole house of Israel," whereas in the Lord's Prayer "Israel," hardly coincidentally, is not mentioned. The most serious difference, namely, the understanding of the kingdom or rule of God, is not evident in the text; rather, it can be discerned only if we see the Lord's Prayer in the context of Jesus' message of the kingdom of God which is approaching and is already dawning (see chap. 5).

Also instructive is the comparison with the most important Jewish prayer, the so-called Eighteen Benedictions. The beginnings of this prayer also go far back, but it was later supplemented and expanded.

Among the eighteen great petitions, one finds those petitions which seek the forgiveness of sin, deliverance, return home of exiles, and assembly of Israel; but one also finds the desire for the punishment of slanderers and evildoers. Much more could be cited from the rich treasury of prayers in Judaism; the fine collection *Gottesdienst des Herzens* (Worship of the heart), by J. Petuchowski, should be mentioned.[7] Without doubt Jesus was deeply rooted in the piety and practice of prayer of his people. From his childhood Jesus was familiar with the psalms and other prayers; he prayed them and made them his own. He took part in worship in the synagogue and traveled to Jerusalem to the great festivals. But his own relationship to God and his message of God's kingdom gave his words about God and his prayer to God a peculiar character. That is also evident in the prayer he taught his disciples. We will now consider this peculiar and distinct character that gives the Lord's Prayer its originality as *Jesus'* prayer.

Notes

1. Cf. Heinz Schürmann, *Das Gebet des Herrn* (Freiburg im Breisgau, ⁴1981), pp. 31–46.
2. Thus Anton Vögtle, "Das Vaterunser—Ein Gebet für Juden und Christen?" in *Das Vaterunser: Gemeinsames im Beten von Juden und Christen* (Freiburg-Basel-Vienna, 1974), pp. 165–95; here pp. 167f. and 185.
3. Joachim Jeremias, *The Lord's Prayer* (Philadelphia: Fortress Press, 1964), pp. 31–32.
4. Schürmann, *Das Gebet des Herrn*, p. 125.
5. Following Schürmann, *Das Gebet des Herrn*.
6. Alfons Deissler, "Der Geist des Vaterunsers im alttestamentlichen Glauben und Beten," in Vögtle, *Das Vaterunser*, pp. 15–67.
7. Subtitle: *Eine Auswahl aus dem Gebetsschatz des Judentums* (Freiburg-Basel-Vienna, 1981).

5. GOD THE FATHER
AND THE MESSAGE OF
THE KINGDOM OF GOD

THE LORD'S PRAYER OPENS with the simple, familiar address "Father." It reflects a direct, warm, even affectionate devotion to God, plain and simple. In our day when everything has become so problematic, even close personal relationships, the notion of father presents difficulties for many persons. Human fathers often deny their role as fathers. Among young people an opposition has built up against fathers who still claim an authority which those growing up do not understand. This is not always the case, and a change for the good seems to be on the rise. From a different perspective, women in the feminist movement take offense at the overemphasis on the "fatherly" and wish that the maternal characteristics in the image of God might also receive attention. This demand is justified when the Old Testament is read carefully. Images of maternal love are often attributed to God. "Can a woman forget her sucking child, that she should have no compassion on the son of her womb? Even these may forget, yet I will not forget you" (Isa. 49:15). "As one whom his mother comforts, so I will comfort you" (Isa. 66:13).

It is good to remember that we may always speak of God only analogously, in a way that reflects earthly, human perspectives. But we shall see that speaking about God as Father has a longer tradition in Judaism. Why did Jesus adopt this manner of speech? With good intentions the tone Jesus employed in this address can be easily grasped. When I asked the participants in my Bible study in Melbourne what they felt about the address "Father," only positive responses were given, even by persons from simple cultures.

It is not very encouraging that in a discussion of an ecumenical version of the Lord's Prayer coming to agreement on the address was not easy. Because some in their ecclesiastical tradition pray "Father our" (*Vater unser*) and others "Our Father" (*Unser Vater*), in the end someone had to yield. The earlier German version, "thou who art in heaven," which places too much emphasis on God's place in heaven, could be changed to the shorter "Our Father in heaven." The proposal to say only "Father," as it appears in Luke, corresponding to a more familiar way of speaking, was never adopted (unfortunately). But because emotional factors and subsequent experiences are at work in prayer, we do not want to argue over them if we simply remain faithful to Jesus' intent. But what was Jesus' understanding of God?

JESUS' IDEA OF GOD

Some observations on this were mentioned in our discussion of the Sermon on the Mount; but we must examine more closely how Jesus was rooted in the faith of his people and what appears in his relationship to God as peculiar and unique.

The Traditional View of God

Jesus adopted the unique view of God held by Israel, which understood itself to be chosen by Yahweh and to be his covenant people, and he presupposed it in all his preaching. God is the creator by whose hand everything was brought forth (cf. Mark 10:6) and who preserves and maintains his creation (cf. Matt. 6:25–30). He contains all things (Matt. 5:34) and penetrates everything with his wisdom. He is the God of Israel, the God of its fathers: the God of Abraham, Isaac, and Jacob, a God of the living (Mark 12:26). The confession, "Hear, O Israel: The LORD our God is one LORD; and you shall love the LORD your God with all your heart, and with all your soul, and with all your might" (the Shema), which the pious Israelite recited mornings and evenings, was also declared by Jesus to be the first and great commandment (Mark 12:29f.). God is Lord of history. Without that conception Jesus' message of the kingdom of God would be incomprehensible.

The view, once widespread, that the God of love and mercy that we see in Jesus is in contrast with the overbearing God of the Old Testament, is not defensible. In Ex. 34:6 we read: "The LORD passed before him [Moses], and proclaimed, 'The LORD, the LORD, a God merciful and gracious, slow to anger, and abounding in steadfast love and faithfulness, keeping steadfast love for thousands, forgiving iniquity and transgression and sin, but who will by no means clear the guilty, visiting the iniquity of the fathers upon the children and the children's children, to the third and the fourth generation.'" The proclamation of the Ten Commandments (the Decalogue) is basically grounded in God's salvific activity toward Israel: "I am the LORD your God, who brought you out of the land of Egypt, out of the house of bondage" (Ex. 20:2; also Deut. 5:6). God's liberating act, his demonstration of grace to Israel, precedes the issuance of his commandments. Thus even here, as in the Sermon on the Mount, difficult demands are not simply made but are given as Israel's response to the anticipated activity of its God of the covenant. Therein lies the indissoluble tie of biblical morality to the idea of God; there is a continuous line from the Old Testament to Jesus' message. The God of the Old Testament who elects, rescues, demands, and forgives is none other than the God proclaimed by Jesus. Jesus also accepts the salvation-historical thought of the prophets that, in spite of all breaches of faith, wantonness, and sins of the Israelites, Yahweh turns again and again to his chosen people with mercy.

The idea of the *Father* is also deeply rooted in the thought of Israel. Already in the prophet Hosea (ca. 750 B.C.) we read, "When Israel was a child, I loved him, and out of Egypt I called my son. . . . I led them with cords of compassion, with the bands of love, and I became to them as one who eases the yoke on their jaws, and I bent down to them and fed them (Hos. 11:1ff.). In the postexilic prophecy we read, "Look down from heaven and see, . . . For thou art our Father, though Abraham does not know us and Israel does not acknowledge us; thou, O LORD, art our Father, our Redeemer from of old is thy name" (Isa. 63:15f.). God's fatherly love, which also bears motherly characteristics, is also seen in the lives of individual Israelites, as becomes clear in the piety of the psalms. In the wisdom literature the righteous son of God is mentioned (Wisd. Sol. 2:16ff.; 5:5). The book of *Jubilees,* which comes from the second century B.C., takes up the prophecy of Hos. 2:1: "I shall be their Father and they shall be my children, they will all be called children of the living God" (*Jub.* 1:24f.).

Jesus' listeners were thus able to note with inner assent and joy when he spoke to them of "your (heavenly) Father," one who gives them good things, more and with greater certainty than earthly fathers are prepared to give their children (Matt. 7:9–11). They also had to be responsive when he demanded of them, "Be merciful, even as your Father is merciful" (Luke 6:36). The prayer to the Father in heaven, the Father of Israel, was also familiar to them from their prayers. Their hearts had to be warmed when Jesus described to them God's care for the birds of the air and the lilies of the field and his still greater concern for people (Matt. 6:25–30). For Jewish listeners, the whole Sermon on the Mount, insofar as it reflects the traditional sayings of Jesus, was nothing strange or incomprehensible; rather, it was something attractive and, at the same time, challenging. They knew this God whom Jesus proclaimed, and yet they did not know him as Jesus presented him to them. It was a new revelation of God for them. We will now turn to this new and original character in Jesus' proclamation of God.

God the Father—Jesus' Particular View

In a groundbreaking study Joachim Jeremias has called attention to the unique address "Abba" used by Jesus.[1] The Hebrew *abi* ("my Father") had not been common in popular speech. The Aramaic *abba* is the familiar address of a small child to his or her father (similar to *imma*, "mother"). But this familiar address was also used by grown children toward their father. Wherever rabbis spoke of God as Father, they added "heavenly" because, for them, the familiar, intimate address of "Father" for God seemed disrespectful. Jeremias established that addressing God as Abba is without analogy in all of Jewish prayer literature.

There are clear indications that Jesus employed this familiar address of Abba for God. On the Mount of Olives, according to the portrayal of the evangelists, he prays, "Abba, Father, all things are possible to thee; remove this cup from me; yet not what I will, but what thou wilt" (Mark 14:36 par.; cf. also John 12:27f.). Here the Aramaic word is retained and is translated into Greek by Mark for his readers.

Certainly one can object that the disciples, who were somewhat removed, were unable to hear the prayer directly; but the unanimous tradition leads at least to the conclusion that the disciples were aware of this familiar address of God that Jesus customarily used. How can one otherwise explain the striking Aramaic word that the evangelists retain? This Aramaic Abba was also incorporated into the prayer language of the primitive church. In two places Paul uses it: Gal. 4:6: "God has sent the Spirit of his Son into our hearts, crying, 'Abba! Father!'"; and Rom. 8:15f.: "For you did not receive the spirit of slavery to fall back into fear, but you have received the spirit of sonship. When we cry, 'Abba! Father!' it is the Spirit himself bearing witness with our spirit that we are children of God." This peculiar, special address to God was taken up by the primitive church and reflects Jesus' instructions on prayer. Christian prayer is prayer in the Holy Spirit, which welcomes Christians into the intimate and confident relationship of Jesus to God.

On the other hand, the synoptic tradition indicates that Jesus himself spoke of God and to God as "Father," in what was for him a reserved way. In many statements he speaks to the disciples of "your Father"; only in the Lord's Prayer does he teach the disciples to address God as Abba. In this prayer he allows his disciples to participate in his relationship to God. Jeremias says, "One may conclude that the delivery of the Lord's Prayer to the disciples signified the warrant to use Abba."[2]

Many traditional sayings of Jesus attest that he wanted to bring the disciples into a close, intimate relationship to God. For the most part we know them from the Sermon on the Mount. The Gospel of Mark, which does not contain the text of the Lord's Prayer, also offers such suggestions. We are reminded of the texts with which we began, especially the statement about prayer: "Therefore I tell you, whatever you ask in prayer, believe that you have received it, and it will be yours" (Mark 11:24).

Even the texts in John regarding the assured favorable hearing on prayer (John 14:13; 15:7; 16:23) appear in this light like an echo. Jesus' high-priestly prayer (John 17) is, to be sure, an intercession by Jesus for the disciples, but at the same time it is an encouragement to pray in the same spirit to the Father. At another place he promises them: On that day when he is with the Father, he will no longer pray for them, for the Father himself loves them and will hear them (John 16:26f.). It appears that in Jesus' farewell prayer, motifs of the Lord's Prayer also resonate (hallowing of God's name, protection from evil).[3]

However, this fatherly image of God does not lack characteristics of exaltation. God remains Lord of heaven and earth, everything remains subject to his will (Matt. 11:25f.). In the Lord's Prayer immediately following the invocation to the Father we find the petition, "Hallowed be thy name." As in the prophets, Jesus' great desire that God's name "become great" is shown in his power and glory before all nations. "Then they will know that I am the Lord GOD" (Ezek. 28:23–25). It is an all-encompassing petition that stands above all petitions in the Lord's Prayer, praise and petition combined into one. Jesus' prayer in John 12:28 illustrates how this "opening petition" (Heinz Schürmann) is best to be understood: "Father, glorify thy name." Thus God is to reveal himself in his greatness and power. With the same words Israel praises God's activity in history and prays for final liberation from all distress and slavery (cf. the Kaddish).

But Jesus directs the petition to the Father. The Father, who now already reveals his kingdom mercifully toward human beings, is now to establish it in the world and finally to fulfill it in the coming kingdom. Thus the arc spans from the idea of the Father to the message of God's kingdom as Jesus proclaims it—as already dawning and as a future expectation. If we with Jesus pray that God's name be hallowed, the will must be awakened within us to meet with open hearts the Father who is open to our petitions. We must bear in mind the demands of the Sermon on the Mount if we present this petition to the Father.

THE MESSAGE OF
THE KINGDOM OF GOD

If the central concern of the Lord's Prayer is the petition for God's kingdom to come, it must be closely tied to the idea of Father. This God to whom worshipers turn with the confident address "Father" should and will establish his liberating and happy rule. This notion also has deep roots in the Old Testament and early Judaism.

The Jewish Legacy

In the ancient Song of Moses, which followed the deliverance from the Red Sea by the annihilation of the Egyptian forces (although it was composed later), we read at the end, "The LORD will reign for ever and ever" (Ex. 15:18). Yahweh has shown himself to be a companion with his people, their commander and aid, and will continue to do so. The memory of this act of liberation has never been lost among the people of Israel and forms the basis of faith in the kingship of God. The Gentile seer Baalam says, "He has not beheld misfortune in Jacob; nor has he seen trouble in Israel. The LORD their God is with them, and the shout of a king is among them" (Num. 23:21; cf. 24:7).

The original meaning, then, is not a kingdom that God establishes but rather his kingly rule which is reflected in the history of Israel. The ark of the covenant represents God's throne (cf. Num. 10:35f.); it travels beyond Shiloh (1 Sam. 4:4), coming finally to the city of David, Jerusalem (2 Samuel 6). There Solomon builds the magnificent temple as "God's dwelling" (1 Kings 8:6). Under severe threat by the king of Assyria, King Hezekiah prays in the temple in Jerusalem: "O LORD the God of Israel, who art enthroned above the cherubim, thou art the God, thou alone, of all the kingdoms of the earth; thou hast made heaven and earth" (2 Kings 19:15). God's kingship is understood to be universal; since the creation he rules over the earth and protects Israel, his chosen covenant people. His all-encompassing kingly rule is sung even in cultic hymns. "Thy kingdom is an everlasting kingdom, and thy dominion endures throughout all generations" (Ps. 145:13).

In times of distress and exile, which Israel experienced under the dominion of foreign nations, there arises from their faith the hope that God will establish his kingship over Israel again. Although the prophets say little of this "kingship" of Yahweh, no doubt because they strongly criticize the earthly kings in Judah and Israel, the idea itself persists and assumes shape again and again. Thus we read in Micah 4:7 (as the threatening sermon of the ancient prophet was filled with words of comfort after judgment), "and the lame I will make the remnant; and those who were cast off, a strong nation; and the LORD will reign over them in Mount Zion from this time forth and for evermore." In the Babylonian exile this prophecy of the future flourishes and also takes on universal features: the pilgrimage of nations to Zion (Isa. 2:2–4; Micah 4:1–4), peace in the creation (Isa. 11:6–8; 35:1–10; Ezek. 34:25–27; et al.), God's banquet on Mount Zion for all nations (Isa. 25:6–8). Jesus also employed such images for the coming kingdom of God (Matt. 8:11; images of the harvest and of the banquet).

Jesus pays most attention to the prophecy of salvation in the second and third parts of Isaiah. For example, the image of the messenger of joy, who hurries ahead to those returning from Babylon and announces liberation and happiness to the city of Jerusalem, is taken up in the "gospel," God's message of joy which Jesus proclaims (cf. Mark 1:15). "How beautiful upon the mountains are the feet of him who brings good tidings, who publishes peace, who brings good tidings of good, who publishes salvation, who says to Zion, 'Your God reigns'" (Isa. 52:7). In the view of the primitive church the messenger of joy (in Greek the same root word as "gospel") was Jesus, and with this interpretation it certainly conveys what Jesus announces, what is reflected in his work, and what he himself intends. According to Luke 4:18–21, Jesus takes the words from Isa. 61:1f. to refer to himself: "The Spirit of the Lord is upon me, because he has anointed me to preach good news to the poor. He has sent me to proclaim release to the captives and re-covering of sight to the blind, to set at liberty those who are oppressed, to proclaim the acceptable year of the Lord." In the Beatitudes we saw how close these words come to the words delivered by Jesus. This prophetic message was fulfilled in his person; in his time ("today") the time of salvation began.

For Israel there remains a constant hope that God will "bring his kingdom to rule . . . quickly and soon" (Kaddish). In the new year Musaph prayer we read, "Then wilt thou rule alone, Lord our God, over all thy creatures in Mount Zion, thy holy city."[4] Universal features such as the expansion of divine rule over all nations of the earth are not lacking here either; thus, in another prayer that was originally offered at the new year festival (when one remembered especially God's king-ship) we read, "So we hope, Lord our God, to see soon the glorification of thy power, when idolatry vanishes from the earth and idols are de-stroyed, when the world is improved through the kingdom of the Almighty."[5]

The notion that God's kingly rule will be established in all the world by his power has thus lived in Israel since ancient times and has persisted in Judaism to this day. It took various forms depending on the different directions within Judaism (in Qumran, in Pharisaism and rab-binicalism, in apocalypticism, etc.); we cannot go into that here. But there can be no doubt that Jesus grew up in this spiritual climate and was affected by the longing of his nation.

The Particular Message of Jesus

Jesus announces the accomplished rule of God as imminent; his message is rooted in this eschatological perspective which is directed at the end and the consummation. "The kingdom of God is at hand" (Mark 1:15). There are even some sayings that appear to limit this com-ing temporally (in the generation still living) (Mark 9:1 par.; 13:30 par.; Matt. 10:23); but these could reflect actual interpretations in primitive Christian communities.[6] Jesus himself leaves the specific time to the sovereign will of God (cf. Mark 13:32 par.; Luke 17:20f.) as he places all things in the power of God (cf. Mark 10:38–40). But he prophetically and penetratingly presents to his hearers a vision of the speedy coming of God, or the "Son of man," even for judgment, as an admonition and a warning. This becomes sufficiently clear from the frequent challenges to "watch and be ready" and from the sayings and parables that require an immediate decision in the light of the threatening judgment (cf. Luke 17:26–30; "crisis parables" such as Luke 16:1–8; Matt. 24:43f., 45–52; and others).[7] The meaning of these statements from tradition is not the announcement of judgment as such but rather the demand to take advantage of God's offer of grace here and now. With that we come to the center of Jesus' proclamation of God's kingdom.

In his work in the present Jesus saw the final kingdom of God which culminates in his end-time coming. That is the main difference from the Jewish faith, the special character of Jesus' preaching: Now God's kingdom breaks in with noticeable power. It is announced in Jesus' casting out of demons (Luke 11:20/Matt. 12:28), it is seen in his healings (Matt. 11:5/Luke 7:22), but it is also expressed in his teaching with authority (Mark 1:22) and in his message of salvation for the poor and the oppressed (cf. the Beatitudes).

Is that perhaps only the view of the primitive church, which evaluated Jesus' work retrospectively from its faith in Christ? But there are indisputable statements by Jesus that reveal his firm conviction: What the prophets once promised in their view of the future has now become reality: "Blessed are the eyes which see what you see! For I tell you that many prophets and kings desired to see what you see, and did not see it, and to hear what you hear, and did not hear it" (Luke 10:23–24; cf. Matt. 13:16f.). What happened in Jesus' present had to lead all persons to conversion. "For the queen of the South . . . came from the ends of the earth to hear the wisdom of Solomon, and behold, something greater than Solomon is here. The men of Nineveh will arise at the judgment with this generation and condemn it; for they repented at the preaching of Jonah, and behold, something greater than Jonah is here" (Luke 11:31f./Matt. 12:41f.). In the "violence saying," which is certainly not uniformly received in tradition, we read, "From the days of John the Baptist until now the kingdom of heaven has suffered violence, and men of violence take it by force" (Matt. 11:12; cf. Luke 16:16). In spite of the darkness of this saying, it expresses the certainty that a new time has now dawned.

In spite of their disputed interpretation, even the "growth parables" of the sower, of the seed that springs up on its own, of the mustard seed (Mark 4), of weeds among the wheat (Matt. 13:24–30), and other parables reflect the fact that for Jesus the kingdom of God is already a power at work in the present. Finally, its present reality is tied to Jesus' self-understanding that through him and his activity God intends and brings to reality something new. As discreetly as Jesus expresses himself about his own person, he is just as certain that God announces his salvific will and carries out his vivid acts of salvation through him.

With that we come to a second characteristic of Jesus' proclamation of God's kingdom: It is a liberating and happy fact that is grounded in God's mercy. Jesus announced as an already present reality that which was alive and remained alive in Israel as a hope for the future, the deliverance of Israel from all distress and oppression. This salvific will of God becomes visible in God's unconditional readiness to forgive which Jesus imparts in a word of forgiveness, even to the despised tax collectors and prostitutes (Mark 2:5; Luke 7:48; Matt. 21:31). There are, in addition, his "symbolic activities," such as eating with the tax collector,[8] as well as other statements and parables (Matt. 18:23–35; Luke 15:11–32). God's mercy encounters the "lost son" in the father in the parable of the prodigal son. As already seen, this mercy is already present before a person is summoned to a corresponding conduct.

This leads to a third feature of Jesus' proclamation: With a decisiveness similar to that with which he announces God's mercy, he demands of those who listen to his sermon that they practice mercy and love even toward the most marginalized persons. Thus, the kingdom of God takes on an obligatory dimension that defines one's actions. The close connection between message and demand was seen in the Sermon on the Mount. It is strengthened by many texts outside the Sermon on the Mount; we need think only of the picture of the final judgment that Matthew paints (Matt. 25:31–46).

Jesus' proclamation of God's kingdom is a uniform view that is based on his idea of God; that view is far more than a "teaching," a collection of statements. It is a lively unity out of which arise new impulses for faith and life.

Present and Future

As the great petition "Thy kingdom come" stands, without doubt it refers, above all, to the future fulfilled kingdom of God. In many other of Jesus' statements that is also the central thrust, the baseline perspective toward which everything moves, the great expectation and promise. Besides being found in images of the harvest, the feast, the growing tree (Mark 4:32), and others that by their application in the Old Testament point to future fulfillment, it is also frequently expressed in the form of "entering the kingdom of God" (Mark 9:47; 10:15, 23; Matt. 7:21; etc.) or of "inheriting eternal life" (Mark 10:17; cf. Matt. 5:5). But if God's kingdom is already "coming," embedded in the petition also is the desire that God's rule be realized in this time, in our world as far as possible. Not to be ignored is the wish that is added or that "clarifies" in Matthew: "Thy will be done on earth as it is in heaven." And if the petitions in the second part still stand under the overarching idea of the coming kingdom, then simply by the fact that they are there and are fervently extolled it becomes clear that God's kingdom, which is still not present in its fullness, nevertheless can and should be perceptible and active even now. It is a dynamic event that encompasses present and future, the present with its call and challenge to human beings; the earthly future as God's future which is illuminated by God's powers and human efforts, the final future which brings human history to its end and goal, but only as a future which arises out of God's will and power. It is a view of history that under the idea of God extends from the creation to the new creation. Then will he who sits on the throne say, "Behold, I make all things new" (Rev. 21:5). In the light of this goal, but still in the midst of ongoing history with all its darkness and suffering, the passionate petition is raised: Thy kingdom come.

Notes

1. "Abba," in Joachim Jeremias, *Abba: Studien zur neutestamentlichen Theologie und Zeitgeschichte* (Göttingen, 1966), pp. 15–67.

2. Ibid., p. 65.

3. Cf. Wilhelm Thüsing, "Die Bitten des johanneischen Jesus in dem Gebet Joh 17 und die Intentionen Jesu von Nazaret," in *Die Kirche des Anfangs* (Festschrift für Heinz Schürmann) (Freiburg-Basel-Vienna, 1978), pp. 307–37.

4. J. Petuchowski, *Gottesdienst des Herzens: Eine Auswahl aus dem Gebetsschatz des Judentums* (Freiburg-Basel-Vienna, 1981), p. 79.

5. Ibid., pp. 80f.

6. Cf. Lorenz Oberlinner, "Die Stellung der 'Terminworte' in der eschatologischen Verkündigung des Neuen Testaments," in *Gegenwart und kommendes Reich,* ed. P. Fiedler and D. Zeller (Stuttgart, 1975), pp. 51–66.

7. Cf. Joachim Jeremias, *The Parables of Jesus* (London: SCM Press, 1962), pp. 169–80.

8. Cf. Maria Trautmann, *Zeichenhafte Handlungen Jesu: Ein Beitrag zur Frage nach geschichtlichen Jesus,* Forschung zur Bibel 37 (Würzburg, 1980).

6. GOD'S KINGDOM AND THE ABIDING NEEDS OF OUR EARTHLY EXISTENCE

IF JESUS IS CHARACTERIZED as "utopian" or visionary because of his extreme demands in the Sermon on the Mount, we learn differently in the second part of the Lord's Prayer. Here he shows himself to be a realist who does not lose sight of reality. Jesus' view of earthly and historical reality goes beyond his own tradition. His heart is open to the needs of simple people. His healings testify to that, as does his attention to those who are troubled by worries. Many statements reveal his understanding of what is necessary for life. When large crowds had followed him to a lonely place, although he wanted to be alone with his disciples, we read, "As he went ashore he saw a great throng, and he had compassion on them, because they were like sheep without a shepherd" (Mark 6:34). What follows is the feeding of the five thousand.

This "compassion" or "mercy" of Jesus has various aspects In the view of the evangelists—two dimensions, as it were. It can be understood as an expression for the momentary external need of persons who are hungry after a long excursion without enough food. In the second account of the feeding of the multitude we read, "I have compassion on the crowd, because they have been with me now three days, and have nothing to eat; and if I send them away hungry to their homes, they will faint on the way; and some of them have come a long way" (Mark 8:2f.). Perhaps this is even the older account (the feeding of the four thousand). But in the other depiction, Mark interprets Jesus' "mercy" further with the quotation, "They were like sheep without a shepherd" (Ezek. 34:5): Behind the external need stands the aimlessness, the lack of orientation of people who despair in a deeper sense. In the speech of the prophet Ezekiel (chapter 34), God turns mercifully to the scattered sheep of his fold, the people of Israel who have been left in the lurch by their leaders. In the description of God's care for his deserted herd there also appears the promise that he will provide for them a simple shepherd who will lead them to pasture, "my servant David" (Ezek. 34:23f.). Jesus is this messianic shepherd who espouses the cause of the people.

Both aspects are joined together in the petitions of the Lord's Prayer: concern for earthly needs, the essentials for subsistence, and concern for the spiritual health of the individual, for that which is most necessary for life. It is the personal existence of individuals out of which their entire life becomes bright and whole, meaningful and happy. The first is treated in the petition for bread, the second particularly in the petition for forgiveness of debts. Both are taken up and encompassed in the petition not to be led into temptation. For do not the external existential needs and the internal threat by the power of evil, which gives rise to anxiety, also become a salvation-threatening "temptation" to the individual? Jesus seems to consider the latter to be a greater threat because the sinister power of evil, which darkens the present and clouds the future, envelops in profound darkness the personal existence of the individual and the historical situation of humanity. In Jesus' view not only are those peoples who live on the edge of dignified human existence threatened, but equally as much, if not more so, are the wealthy nations with their luxury and abundance threatened by a total human catastrophe. However, we cannot dissociate the two from each other, nor can we tear asunder bodily needs from emotional, spiritual needs. Jesus, the realist, looks at both, each in itself and the two bound together, as a dangerous avalanche that is advancing toward humanity.

Can human beings stop this avalanche? Jesus teaches us to ask God the Father to have mercy in all this distress and to protect us from the abyss. In his unshakable trust Jesus is convinced that God can do it. As he teaches us this prayer and wants to draw us into this same trust, he also calls us to do what is possible, to do what is necessary for ourselves and all of humanity. We are able to resist all distress, threat, and doubt because we cling to God's power and his promise that he wishes to establish his kingdom in this world now and someday bring it to fulfillment.

But now let us examine the petitions individually.

THE PETITION FOR BREAD

Examined closely, the familiar formulation "Give us this day our daily bread" is a combination of the Matthean and Lukan versions. For that reason it is one-dimensional for us because we eat bread daily for nourishment and also need it as the most important food (in spite of all the diet programs). In ancient Palestine that was beyond question; bread was prepared and baked daily (as flat cakes). From the parable in Luke 11:5–8 one may conclude that three such bread cakes were desired in order to have a satisfactory meal. The need for bread had therefore to be met daily. The petition to give us bread "today" (Matthew) can then mean to give it to us in a timely way, perhaps even today for tomorrow. In contrast, the Lukan version "each day" sounds somewhat refined. An exegetical difficulty is found in the Greek adjective added by both evangelists to "bread" (*ton epiousion*), which except for a dubious place in a papyrus is otherwise not evident anywhere.[1] Neither the attempts to translate back into Aramaic nor derivations from the Greek have led to clear results. Did the original text read, "Give us today our bread for tomorrow"? Or, "Give us today [or: daily] the bread which is important and necessary"? According to most more recent interpreters, however, the meaning of the bread petition is not affected by this uncertainty. It is a petition for the bread that we need, the necessary bread that God may give us today (and tomorrow) and daily.

The possible original version, "Give us today our bread for tomorrow," has also led to another interpretation that has become common: The "bread for tomorrow" is understood as the end-time feast, an image for the future kingdom of God (cf. Luke 14:15). The meaning of the petition would then be: Bring the perfected kingdom of God soon ("today"), give us the bread of the time of salvation, the bread of life.[2] In fact, this interpretation in the ancient church, in the East as well as in the West, was widespread. This also brought to mind the manna which became a symbol for the true bread of life. Jean Carmignac combines a series of these interpretations and expresses his view that from the petition for bread one ought to hear equally a request for bodily nourishment, for God's word, and for the Eucharist.[3]

But as interesting as such interpretations may be for meditation, they go beyond the original meaning and depart from the hard reality for which this petition achieves a constantly new actuality. They deprive the bread petition of something of its original emphasis and weaken the idea, with which we would not like to dispense, regarding Jesus' proximity to human beings and his humanity. Jesus wants to say to us: The Father who has given himself to human beings knows what you need and wants you to ask him for it.

If we consider the situation of Jesus' disciples who had left house and home for Jesus' sake, we understand that with this petition Jesus wanted to instill in them an enormous confidence in times of need. For the charismatic itinerant preachers who after Jesus' death went out in great frugality to announce God's kingdom to the people of Israel it was a sign that Jesus was thinking of what was necessary for life with which even they could not dispense. The instructions read: They are to accept openly what people offer them in their itinerant mission work. "Whenever you enter a town and they receive you, eat what is set before you" (Luke 10:8). A general statement is also cited: "The laborer deserves his wages" (Luke 10:7).

Here it is evident that the petition for bread also has a social function. Again and again it calls to mind God's will that all persons receive their daily bread (or, in other countries, their bowl of rice). In our day, when hunger in the world daily takes the lives of countless persons, particularly children, it becomes a constant challenge to the haves and the well-fed to share bread with the hungry and the starving.

If the early church elevated the bread petition to its prayer in the Eucharist, that is an application to the believing community gathered for the Lord's Supper. And yet, in partaking in the Eucharistic bread it did not forget the earthly bread that every person seeks. The Lord's Supper became an admonition to remember the poor and the needy in the community. For a long time there was the custom of feeding or supporting the needy with gifts brought to the altar; and beyond that there were love feasts (*agapē*) at which bodily and spiritual hunger were to be simultaneously appeased. In our day, collections during the worship service that are intended not only for members of the community but also for the hungry peoples in the world have taken over this function. The awareness that receiving and giving, divine gifts and human sharing, and "heavenly" and earthly bread belong together can also lead in our churches to a deeper understanding of what Jesus intended in the Lord's Prayer.

THE PETITION FOR FORGIVENESS

In Aramaic, guilt and sin are included under the idea of debts; for his Greek readers Luke changes it to "sins." Jesus tells several parables about debts, such as the parable of the two debtors (Luke 7:41–43) and the parable of the unforgiving servant (Matt. 18:23–35). Before God we are all debtors, burdened with enormous, innumerable debts. That is difficult for people today to accept, and yet this is the basic situation of all of humanity before God; indeed, it is the foundation of our understanding of existence. If human beings do not recognize that they do not have themselves to thank for everything they have and are able to do, they develop an attitude of self-certainty, pride, and arrogance that blinds them to their limitations, their dependence on other persons and on the society in which they find themselves. Out of this there arise those misguided attitudes and lapses toward neighbors and the social order which we call offenses against custom, infringements of the law, crimes, or, in a comprehensive sense, "sins." To these also belong omissions of the good that we owe our fellow citizens. So the denial of our guilt before God also affects relations of human beings with one another.

Paul says, "All have sinned and fall short of the glory of God" (Rom. 3:23); but he also continues, "they are justified by his grace as a gift, through the redemption which is in Christ Jesus." Jesus also saw all human beings as sinners before God. Characteristic of that is the scene Luke describes: "There were some present at that very time who told him of the Galileans whose blood Pilate had mingled with their sacrifices. And he answered them, 'Do you think that these Galileans were worse sinners than all the other Galileans, because they suffered thus? I tell you, No; but unless you repent you will all likewise perish. Or those eighteen upon whom the tower of Siloam fell and killed them, do you think that they were worse offenders than all the others who dwelt in Jerusalem? I tell you, No; but unless you repent you will all likewise perish'" (Luke 13:1–5).

Jesus addressed such actual occasions to make people of that time aware that all are sinners and need to repent. All of us must also pray, "Forgive us our sins." However, to those who ask this of the Father humbly he also proclaims forgiveness of all guilt out of God's free goodness and mercy.

But the Lord's Prayer looks not only at the single, fundamental change in attitude and repentance that everyone needs but also at the more far-reaching sins. In God's mercy, which is available to everyone, we must constantly seek anew forgiveness of our sins. God's further forgiving goodness is also available to us. That is seen most beautifully in the forgiveness Jesus grants Peter after his denial (cf. Luke 22:32; John 21:15–17). Repentance and conversion are the purification bath that brings us again to reconciliation with God and to peace. So the petition for forgiveness becomes a call to self-examination because only in confession of our guilt may we hope to enter the kingdom of God. To the unrepentant in Israel, Jesus says, "Truly, I say to you, the tax collectors and the harlots go into the kingdom of God before you" (Matt. 21:31).

When, following the petition for forgiveness, we assure God that we have also released our debtors from their debts (so Matthew), or when we say, "as we also forgive the one who is indebted to us," i.e., the one who has made himself or herself guilty toward us (so Luke), that is not meant as a condition for God to forgive us. God forgives us on his own, graciously and unconditionally, but he *expects* us also to forgive those who have sinned against us. In prayer we assure God that we are ready to do that when we turn to him, having already forgiven our neighbor (Matthew) or forgiving the neighbor in this hour (Luke). Again and again we must be ready to forgive, as Jesus' answer to Peter makes clear (Matt. 18:21f.). But with Peter and the primitive church we see how difficult that is. It is not easy to pray the Lord's Prayer honestly; it is an exorbitant challenge.

That brings the petition for forgiveness, with the addition of our human promise, very close to the Sermon on the Mount. Here it becomes immediately clear that our prayers to the almighty and merciful Father always include and call forth our own efforts as well. Prayer is not a flight into nonresponsibility or self-consolation with the notion that God will take everything that we cannot do and make it good.

Our pledge to God has a particular urgency in the light of today's efforts for peace between persons and among nations. All peace begins with reconciliation, and reconciliation presupposes forgiveness. Although we cannot with certainty bring about grace with our willingness to forgive, we can create a necessary condition for it. Not all questions of creating peace and keeping peace are thereby resolved; but the call to reconciliation remains unmistakable (cf. Luke 12:58f.). Matthew sharpened that call for his community, in which there were obstinate and sinful members. Following the Lord's Prayer he formulates it as a real condition: "For if you forgive men their trespasses, your heavenly Father also will forgive you; but if you do not forgive men their trespasses, neither will your Father forgive your trespasses" (Matt. 6:14f.)

The petition for forgiveness concerns our salvific situation, which is grounded in God; however we use it, we will one day have to answer to God. Finally, at stake is the divine judgment to which every person is subject. But the petition is set in the present time and also takes into account the constantly recurring trespasses of Jesus' disciples. Again we see Jesus' realism in that he is aware of the ongoing weakness and fresh lapses of his disciples. Again and again God is ready to forgive our sins. The question of the hereditary character of sin was dealt with by the primitive church with growing seriousness. The authority of Jesus to bind and to loose (Matt. 16:19; 18:18) is applied in the statement by the risen Lord in John 20:23 regarding the forgiveness of sins: "If you forgive the sins of any, they are forgiven; if you retain the sins of any, they are retained."

In 1 John, which comes to terms with false teachers who considered themselves above sinfulness, the Christians are told, "If we say we have no sin, we deceive ourselves, and the truth is not in us" (1 John 1:8). But God's desire to forgive is proclaimed anew: "If we confess our sins, he is faithful and just, and will forgive our sins and cleanse us from all unrighteousness" (1 John 1:9).

Various paths to forgiveness of sins also become evident: "If any one does sin, we have an advocate with the Father, Jesus Christ the righteous" (1 John 2:1). We are also able to intercede for a brother who has sinned: "and God will give him life for those whose sin is not mortal" (1 John 5:16). Sin is taken seriously as a power that separates us from God and that can also lead to spiritual death; but the writer is likewise convinced that "the evil one" is not truly capable of harming the children of God (1 John 5:18). The Lord's Prayer, which Jesus taught his disciples, reflects this serious view of sin as well as this confidence in a merciful and faithful God. In the wide-ranging statements in 1 John, a sliver of Christian life is reflected, but also the unbroken power of confidence.

THE PETITION FOR DELIVERANCE
FROM TEMPTATION

With that we come to the last of the urgent petitions for our earthly-historical existence. We still live in a world that is characterized by an enormous pressure of temptation to evil. "And lead us not into temptation," reads this petition in a literal translation of the Greek. Thoughtful Christians take offense at this formulation, for can God lead into temptation, thus threatening our salvation? That cannot be what is meant; James 1:13 guards against such a misunderstanding: "Let no one say when he is tempted, 'I am tempted by God'; for God cannot be tempted with evil and he himself tempts no one." It is a Semitic expression that means, "And let us not slip into temptation." Paul says, "No temptation has overtaken you that is not common to man. God is faithful, and he will not let you be tempted beyond your strength" (1 Cor. 10:13).

"Temptation" is a word that has various meanings in the New Testament. Upon reflection, the story of Jesus' temptation rings true. Because he is both a human being and "Son of God," he is tempted as is every human being, and yet as "Son of God" he overcomes the temptation. It is an extremely powerful temptation, threatening his life and his salvific work, at the outset of his earthly ministry. Satan, the adversary of God and of the human race, tempts Jesus with cunning words ("if you are God's son") and quotations from scripture in order to divert him from his journey as God's obedient servant. All dangerous temptations in the world are mentioned: material thoughts (earthly goods), exaggerated autonomy (defiance of God), striving for kingdoms (worldly power). In the longer description in the sayings source (Matt. 4:1–11; Luke 4:1–13) the devilish insinuations are also reminiscent of the temptations of Israel in the wilderness. Jesus overcomes all of Satan's attacks by turning attention to God: "Man shall not live by bread alone, but by every word that proceeds from the mouth of God"; "You shall worship the Lord your God and him only shall you serve"; to submit to Satan who offers Jesus all the kingdoms of the world would mean betraying this service which is owed only to God. At the same time, Jesus becomes a unique example of how one overcomes such salvation-threatening temptations: with immediate decisiveness, with orientation to the word of God, with faithfulness to the way that has been paved in service to God.

In the New Testament the temptation situation that threatens our salvation stands in the foreground. Only peripherally do we also hear of tests by "temptations" that can strengthen Christ's disciples and defenders; thus we read in James 1:12, "Blessed is the man who endures trial, for when he has stood the test he will receive the crown of life." Paul speaks of "human," that is, humanly bearable and endurable, temptation (1 Cor. 10:13a). Loss of salvation, falling finally away from faith, is the threatening evil that comes to the disciples of Christ in that "temptation" which is meant in the petition of the Lord's Prayer. In the explanation of the parable of the seed, Luke says of those who "have no roots," "They believe for a while and in time of temptation fall away" (Luke 8:13). Almost like an echo of the petition in the Lord's Prayer is Jesus' statement to the disciples in Gethsemane: "Pray that you may not enter into temptation" (Mark. 14:38 par.).

Behind such a salvation-threatening temptation stands the power of evil. That becomes even clearer in the Matthean expansion "but deliver us from evil." It confirms that by "temptation" is meant a situation in which evil or the evil one can become overwhelming. In the genitive it is not possible to determine whether it is masculine or neuter. In the thought world of the New Testament, evil is embodied in the form of Satan. In another place Matthew also speaks in this way (cf. Matt. 13:19, 38f.). In John 17:15, in Jesus' great prayer to the Father, we find a similar petition: "I do not pray that thou shouldst take them out of the world, but that thou shouldst keep them from the evil one"; and places in 1 John suggest that here also the evil one is in the writer's mind (cf. 1 John 2:13; 5:18). Finally, however, at issue here is not the devil, about whom there are many false ideas. The Christian awareness of the power of the evil one, but also of the overcoming of the evil one, is expressed in the statement, "We know that we are of God, and the whole world is in the power of the evil one" (1 John 5:19).

For Jesus, then, evil is more widespread in the world, active and powerful in ongoing history. In apocalyptically intense depictions the time immediately prior to the end is described not only with increased external tribulations, wars, and natural disasters but also with an accompanying temptation situation. Then tempters, false messiahs, and false prophets will appear, and they will perform signs and wonders "to lead astray, if possible, the elect" (Mark 13:22). Matthew says, "And because wickedness is multiplied, most men's love will grow cold" (Matt. 24:12). Is the temptation from which God is to guard us a situation that appears only at the end of history? But according to other statements by Jesus and the understanding of the primitive church (cf. the above passage from the Johannine writings), all of world history is exposed to the attacks of the evil one. This ongoing threat, real in every hour of world history, not even halting before Jesus' disciples, is what is meant by the "temptation" of which Jesus speaks.

This petition is also a demand, namely, not to make light of the power of evil, not to succumb to those utopias which, only by human reason and human powers, want to remove evil in the world, crime and terror, oppression and war. That does not rule out struggling with evil in all its forms; but the disciple of Christ should know that only God can completely break and overcome the powers of disaster. What he prays for, above all, is that he himself may not be overcome by this power, but he also prays that it may disappear from the world. With justification we translate "deliver us *from* (*von*) the evil one," and not simply "*before* (*vor*) the evil one." But because the prayer is offered in the faith that God's kingdom is coming, fear of the power of evil is eliminated. Prayer to the Father means trusting that he is stronger than the evil powers of destruction and annihilation.

An isolated statement by Jesus reads, "I saw Satan fall like lightning from heaven" (Luke 10:18). The primitive church already saw God's victory won in the cross of Jesus: "Now the salvation and the power and the kingdom of our God and the authority of his Christ have come" (Rev. 12:10). This mood is also present in the concluding doxology, which is most certainly not an original part of the Lord's Prayer but was added early in the ancient church: "For thine is the kingdom and the power and the glory forever. Amen."

Notes

1. Cf. finally Ceslas Spicq, O.P., *Notes de lexicographie néotestamentaire, Supplémentaire,* Orbis Bibl. et Orient. 22/3 (Fribourg-Göttingen, 1982), pp. 292–95.

2. Thus Joachim Jeremias, *The Lord's Prayer* (Philadelphia: Fortress Press, 1964), pp. 23–27. Against this "eschatological" interpretation, cf. Anton Vögtle, "Der 'eschatologische' Bezug der Wir-Bitten des Vaterunser," in *Jesus und Paulus* (Festschrift für Werner Georg Kümmel) (Göttingen, 1975), pp. 344–82.

3. Jean Carmignac, *Recherches sur le "Notre Père"* (Paris: Ed. Letouzey & Ané, 1969), pp. 214–20.

PART 3. TRUST IN TIMES
OF TESTING

TRUST IN TIMES OF TESTING

IF WE LOOK BACK on the Sermon on the Mount and the Lord's Prayer, compare the two texts with each other, and set them in relation to each other, the common basis that supports and makes everything meaningful is confidence in God the Father from which Jesus proclaims, demands, and teaches us to pray and ask. His demands in the Sermon on the Mount can be accepted and fulfilled by one who is prepared to make Jesus' statement his or her own: "All things are possible to the one who believes."

The Lord's Prayer will be voiced in the spirit of Jesus only by those who with Jesus gaze up to the Father whom they address in this prayer, like Jesus, in gentle trust and with the same confidence. Those who do not come to terms with the demands of the Sermon on the Mount must take refuge in this prayer, and those who pray it must always remember what Jesus demands of them in the Sermon on the Mount.

Together, they are a summons and a challenge by which disciples of Jesus are called to accept and, with him, to embody that comprehensive program which resounds in the gospel. Encouragement and promise, demand and call to action are likewise contained in it. Everything is based on what Jesus announced in God's name to the people of that day: "The kingdom of God is at hand; repent and believe the gospel." Everything stands or falls on this message and trust in God the Father who proclaimed it through Jesus.

In our day, after many centuries of the proclamation of the gospel, after many experiences of Christians, often oppressing and disappointing experiences, a final question remains that cannot be avoided. After all the failures of Christians and of nations and governments that call themselves Christian, can we in good conscience still proclaim the Sermon on the Mount? Can we still honestly pray the Lord's Prayer in a time of horrible events ("after Auschwitz") and their present manifestations—in the face of a continuing deterioration of the world situation in spite of all peace efforts, of increasing outbreaks of hatred and hostility, of all the atrocities and murders? Can we still demand the utmost in ethical strictness, with any expectation of success, with the same trust as Jesus did? Can we still pray to the Father with the same confidence that Jesus did? The enormous burden of suffering and of evil that has mounted over the centuries weighs on our shoulders. What is more, the guilt we share with our parents and ancestors is almost overwhelming. Confidence in Jesus and his message is at the breaking point.

With this internal distress which attacks our faith, we can only pray the Lord's Prayer more ardently: Father, forgive us our debts, lead us not into temptation, deliver us from evil, not only from the evil in the world but also from the evil in our own hearts. But when I consider that we are to proclaim the message of the liberating kingdom of God and teach the Lord's Prayer to the oppressed persons and nations, I am led to even greater despair. We must put ourselves in their humanly hopeless situation just once. There are countless persons who live at the edge of existence and do not have even the slightest hope of escaping this mire and suffering, this demonic abyss, in spite of all efforts and labor. And there are nations and groups that with today's concentration of power have surrendered all illusions of achieving a free, dignified life. We, who belong to that small class which has so much, can hardly imagine that. How would we feel if we were among those unfortunate ones? Would we consider it acceptable for someone to tell us, "Only believe, only trust"?

But did not Jesus himself experience this internal distress when he saw that most of his own people refused to believe him, and when his collective movement collapsed? Must not his trust in God have been shaken as he saw suffering and death approaching him? In fact, he was not spared the experience on the Mount of Olives in which the fear of death seized him: "My soul is very sorrowful, even to death" (Mark 14:34). But in his prayer to the Father, he reached a new trust and obedience in this dark hour. On the cross we hear him utter the cry, "My God, my God, why hast thou forsaken me?" (Mark 15:34). We do not know how deep this sense of God-forsakenness was; they are the opening words of a psalm in which one human being cries out, in extreme distress, his doubt in God, but by the end is certain of rescue by God. We must leave standing Jesus' God-forsakenness in its hard, impenetrable reality. Only God can provide the final answer to the darkest problem of human and historical existence "beneath the cross" of the world's suffering and guilt, and God has provided it in the resurrection of the crucified one. That is not a rational, but an existential answer to which we can only in faith say yes. It is an answer that leads to the mystery of God who in his unfathomable love spared not even his own son, but gave himself up for us all (Rom. 8:32).

Trust, as the biblical message teaches us, means not doubting the love of God in spite of the world's hatred and the power of evil. "Who shall separate us from the love of Christ? Shall tribulation, or distress, or persecution, or famine, or nakedness, or peril, or sword? . . . No, in all these things we are more than conquerors through him who loved us" (Rom. 8:35, 37).

INDEX OF REFERENCES

GENERAL INDEX